spin control

spincontrol

Techniques for Spinning the Yarn You Want

amy king

interweavestore.com

Photography, **Joe Coca**
Photo styling, **Ann Swanson**
Process photography, **Ann Swanson**
Art direction and design, **Connie Poole**
Production, **Katherine Jackson**
Technical Editor, **Abby Franquemont**
Editor, **Anne Merrow**

Interweave Press LLC
201 East Fourth Street
Loveland, CO 80537-5655 USA
interweavestore.com

Printed in China by Asia Pacific Offset.

Library of Congress Cataloging-in-Publication Data

King, Amy, 1973-
  Spin control : techniques for spinning the yarn you want / Amy
King.
      p. cm.
  Includes bibliographical references and index.
  ISBN 978-1-59668-105-7
  1. Hand spinning. 2. Spun yarns. I. Title.
  TT847.K563 2009
  746.1'2--dc22

                                2009001063

10 9 8 7 6 5 4 3 2 1

To all spinners of all levels who are making beautiful yarns.

How do I even begin to thank all the people who have helped me create this book?

My husband, Jay, and my two little girls deserve the most thanks of all. They always took it in stride when supper was pizza several nights in a row and even rejoiced when PB&J's was announced as the meal of the night. On top of all that, they listened to me go on and on about this fiber, that wheel, and even when I explained the ins and outs of yarn creation.

My parents deserve a special thank-you for always being there to help and support me—for helping me build my business and for actually learning fiber terms (possibly because when you hear something so many times you can't help but remember some of it), all without complaining and just offering to help more.

Thank you to Anne Merrow, Abby Franquemont, and all of Interweave for believing in me, my book, and generally providing such great resources for us all. Where would we all be without Interweave, which publishes so many of the greatest resources for spinners to learn by?

I want to also thank my friends, who listened to me drone on with fiber information they'd heard so many times or engaged in the same "woolen vs worsted" discussion again and again or dealt with my excited childlike glee at every new publishing experience. Last but not least, I want to thank the Spunquistadores for cheering me on every step of the way.

contents

Be in Control of Your Yarn 9

be in control of your yarn

As spinners, we start with a hunk of fiber and feed it into the orifice of our wheels or onto the shafts of our spindles, and it becomes yarn. With a little more control, technique, and practice, that yarn can be anything we want it to be. Spinners have the potential to make the most gorgeous yarns ever seen. You can make conscious decisions and choices that will give you the yarn that you've been dreaming of—a yarn that you designed and executed.

This book is all about how to be in control of your yarn. Yarns that just "happen"—the happy accidents, the yarns you spin to feel the fiber pass through your fingers—will always have their place, but if you want to make yarn that has been popping up in your dreams or that you just can't find anywhere else, this book will help you get there. While I'm talking about taking more control in your spinning, there are a few techniques that for some of you will be positively freeing. You will get to explore and be wild with your yarns and break out of your limiting spinning habits.

I love everything about yarn, and I want to be able to make any kind I could get commercially as well as any kind that is completely unique to me. That's not to say that a spinner won't ever buy commercial yarns—far from it. It means that we can understand the strengths and weaknesses of millspun yarns and use those qualities to make yarns that complement or contrast with what we can buy.

If you're stuck in a rut, if you have trouble spinning the yarn you really want to knit or weave, if you need to create a handspun to work with a commercial yarn or replace a discontinued one, this book can teach you what you need to know.

There are so many variables when spinning your own yarn and so many yarns to make. With color design, fiber choice, fiber preparation, and spinning techniques, we may live to be one hundred and still not sample every possible yarn. (But I hope you'll try!)

May you spin happy and find joy in all your projects.

spinning techniques

At its most basic, yarn is fiber with twist. From these two factors, there are infinite ways to make yarn and infinite yarns that can result. Creating the specific yarn you want is a matter of matching the type of fiber with the method of spinning that will bring out the characteristics you're after. As you combine fiber and twist in every imaginable way, keeping records of what you've spun and keeping track of a few details can help you make the right yarn every time.

know your fiber

For many of us, fiber is the most seductive part of spinning
. . . the softness of cashmere, sleek shine of silk, or earthy hues of
natural cotton may inspire you to sit down at the wheel. Beyond their
tactile appeal, specific fibers have evolved to make particular yarns
very well.

Knowing the complete history of an animal or breed you are using,
while interesting, isn't necessary for the process of making yarn. You
can get by on knowing the basics, such as texture, staple length, and
color. In addition to the innate properties of fiber, the way it is prepared affects the finished yarn. In this chapter you will learn about
the variety of spinning fibers and how they can become the yarn you
have in mind.

for yourself. The lower the micron count, the finer the fiber is. A higher micron count will let you know that it's a little coarser and the fibers aren't as slippery. The other method of wool grading most commonly used is the English or Spinning Count system, also called the Bradford count, measures the number of skeins that can be spun from a pound of fiber. The higher the number, the finer the wool.

Staple (or fiber length) is an important factor. If you have a fleece, it's easy to pull out a lock and see how long the individual fibers are. To see the staple on prepared top, hold the fiber a few inches from the end, grasp the fiber at the tip, and pull. You'll feel the fibers give way to your tug, and you get a general idea of how long the staple is. You can't do this easily with carded fibers, as the carding generally homogenizes all the fibers, making it difficult to pull out a single staple of fiber. Staple is important because the shorter the fibers, the more twist is needed to hold them together in yarn. The longer the fibers are, the farther apart your hands need to be when drafting so you aren't fighting the fibers to draft.

Factors in Fiber

Texture determines how the yarn will feel, but it also affects how the fiber will behave while spinning. Coarse fibers tend to stick to one another, while finer fibers tend to be more slippery. This comes from the texture of the individual hairs.

If you can't touch the fiber you want, as when you buy over the Internet, it helps if the seller is using a grading system. **Micron count** is a good measure of how your fiber will behave if you can't touch it

Tussah silk

Superwash Corriedale

Color is visual and largely personal. If you are dyeing the fiber, keep in mind that the lighter the base color, the easier it is to achieve the final color you want. Dyeing grays and browns gives interesting results, but it is certainly different from dyeing white fibers. If you have a colored fiber and want white, you cannot bleach it. Bleach will dissolve wool. (I think it's an interesting experiment, if you're willing to waste a little bit of wool.) All three of these fibers were dyed using the same turquoise dye. (The silk required 50 percent more dye to reach the same level of saturation.) Each was prepared as top and then spun as a two-ply worsted yarn. Notice the differences in luster and the texture of the fibers. When planning a garment, keep in mind that the fiber choice will affect the color in the final look.

Romney

Properties of Fiber

What fiber do you want to spin? There are a million choices! Knowing what kind of yarn you need—soft for next-to-skin wear, strong and pill-resistant, cool and machine-washable—will help you decide which fiber (or fibers!) to try for your next project. Fibers fall into three basic classes: natural cellulose, or plant fiber; protein, which is produced by living animals and insects; and man-made fibers, which are transformed by human intervention into spinnable fiber. Each class has shared characteristics, but within each class is more variety than you might imagine.

cellulose	FIBER	TRAITS	USE FOR SPINNERS
cotton	Cotton	Grows on shrubs; commonly white but also available in various natural colors. It can be smooth or harsh, but it's always very short-stapled.	Cotton makes hard-wearing items that do not felt in regular machine-wash cycles. It is common for child or baby garments, kitchen items, or for lightweight warm-weather clothing.
bast	Flax (linen)	Grows as a tall, grassy plant; it is extremely tough and hard wearing and the fibers can be up to 2 feet long. Some kinds of retted flax have shorter staples, which many may find easier to spin. Spinners usually dampen their fingers while drafting so that the fibers lay flat against the yarn. Linen grows softer with use and washing.	Makes fantastic towels and washcloths but can also be made into lovely drapey shells and tank tops.
	Hemp	Fiber similar to flax, but it grows much taller (up to 14 feet) and coarser than flax.	Makes very durable garments and other items.

protein	FIBER	TRAITS	USE FOR SPINNERS
wool	*Fine wools (like Merino and Cormo)*	Incredibly soft, with a short staple, tight crimp, and often an excess of grease (lanolin).	Best used in garments that won't get hard wear (unless you spin them into a tight worsted yarn, which may diminish the softness). These fibers tend to pill and fuzz in a standard yarn but are worth it for the lovely texture.
	Medium wools (like Corriedale and Falkland)	Fairly soft, with a medium staple of usually less than 5 inches and a lot of crimp.	The perfect middle-of-the-road fiber, great for almost any project from mittens and socks to sweaters.
	Long or luster wools (like Romney, Wensleydale, and Border Leicester)	Lustrous and quite strong, with staples up to 12 inches and long, wavy crimp. Can feel hairlike.	These wools make tough, hard-wearing garments such as rugs, socks, and outerwear, though some are soft enough for sweaters, shawls, and scarves as well.
	Primitive wools (like Icelandic and Shetland)	From sheep that generally have at least two coats: a hairy outer layer and a softer inner layer. Once the coats are separated, the inner coat can be as soft and wonderful as many medium or fine wools.	The durable outer coat is best suited for things that may take a beating, such as outerwear or household items such as rugs. The soft inner layers may be used for sweaters, scarves, and other garments that touch the skin.

protein

	FIBER	TRAITS	USE FOR SPINNERS
camelids	*Camel*	Fiber comes from Bactrian camels (the ones with two humps), which have three coats. Handspinners use the softest undercoat, which is downy and short-stapled with a lovely crimp.	Next-to-skin soft and very lightweight, wonderful for undergarments, scarves, lace.
	Alpaca	Comes in huacaya and suri types. Suri fiber is long and silky, while huacaya is woollier. Alpacas come in a wide range of natural colors and often have staples of more than 10 inches. Ranges from next-to-skin soft to slight prickle.	Wonderful in lace and warm drapey garments. Little or no memory; drapes beautifully.
	Llama	Shares traits with both alpaca and camel fibers. Llamas have two coats, an outer hairy one and a soft inner one, with a staple as long as 8–10 inches.	Traditionally spun with guard hair in and used for long-wearing uses such as ropes and bags; can also be dehaired and spun for fine, soft garments.
	Vicuña	Very rare soft fiber from the wild ancestor of the alpaca. The animal is endangered, but some of the downy fiber is legally available in small quantities.	The ultimate luxury fiber, best spun fine. Suited for all luxury applications.
	Guanaco	Down fiber from the wild ancestor of the llama. The luxurious fiber from these endangered animals is rare but available.	Like a less expensive vicuña, best spun fine and used for true luxury purposes.

protein	FIBER	TRAITS	USE FOR SPINNERS
goat fibers	*Mohair (from Angora goats)*	Heavy and tough, with a great shine; it has many traits in common with longwools. Mohair in a blend can greatly increase the yarn's longevity.	Often used in lace yarn because it produces a halo that can increase over time.
	Cashmere	The most readily available luxury fiber. Spinners generally use the downy undercoat, which is crimpy, short-stapled, and incredibly soft.	Wonderful for adding softness to a fiber blend or for making precious small pieces.
angora	*Angora (from French, English, or German rabbits)*	Luxurious, with a super soft yet short and slippery fiber.	Angora is often blended because a little can go a long way toward making plain wool more luxurious. Angora can be used in a wide variety of garments; it makes a very warm yarn, so it's especially nice for things such as mittens, scarves, and hats if you live in a cold clime.
bison, yak, and qiviut	*Bison, Yak, and Qiviut (Musk ox)*	These ancient animals have up to five different coats; the fiber is dehaired to leave the very finest short-staple fiber.	Great blended or used in garments where fuzzy texture, warmth, and a halo are a plus. Used alone and spun very fine, it makes luxurious, extremely warm items.

protein	FIBER	TRAITS	USE FOR SPINNERS
silk	*Bombyx*	Generally considered the finer grade of silk; it is very slippery. Bombyx silkworms are produced only in captivity and are fed a specialized diet. The silk can be "reeled" or drawn off the cocoon in one long, continuous strand. The whitest of silks.	Bombyx makes great blends and is also wonderful used by itself. It's hard wearing, drapes well, and brings shine and a sense of luxury. It lacks the elasticity of wool, so it isn't suited unless blended for items that stretch easily, such as mittens and socks.
	Tussah	Produced both in the wild and in captivity. If a worm has pierced its cocoon and emerged, the strands have been cut. These are then carded, combed into top, or stretched over a group of nails to form hankies and caps. (See page 35 for detail on spinning silk hankies.) Naturally golden in color, sometimes bleached white.	Like bombyx, tussah is great used on its own. It is also available in many commercial blends.
	Silk noil	Fiber left over from the combing and carding process.	Can be carded with other material to produce a tweedy fiber and yarn. Although it can be spun by itself, be prepared for short fibers with lots of little neps (neps or noils are little knots or tuft-like bits of fiber). It can be a challenge to spin unblended noil, but with persistence you can produce an interesting rustic yarn.

man-made	FIBER	TRAITS	USE FOR SPINNERS
regenerated fibers	*Rayon (including Tencel, SeaCell, and bamboo)*	Silk-like long-staple fibers manufactured from vegetable materials.	Can be spun as for silk, but I usually prefer these in blends. Take fiber reactive dyes only.
	Regenerated proteins (including Soy Silk and Silk Latte)	Long-staple fibers made from protein materials (even vegetable proteins). They behave similar to rayons.	Can be blended or spun alone. Take acid dyes.
synthetics	*Nylon*	A man-made isomer of wool, nylon was invented to mimic the natural fiber.	Sometimes spun on its own but more commonly seen in blends, where it adds strength. Takes acid dyes well.
	Firestar	Trilobal Nylon.	Finest of the synthetic glitter fibers, used in blends. Can take acid dyes.
	Angelina	Mylar.	Not dyeable, coarser than Firestar, used in blends.
reclaimed fibers	*Recycled sari silk*	Strands of colorful silk thread or sometimes thin strips of woven fabric left over from the production of clothing.	Spun on its own, sari silk makes a colorful novelty yarn with luster and character. Blended into a batt, it adds shine and interest; depending on the amount of sari silk in the blend, you may spin it as a novelty yarn or more traditionally.
	Recycled blue jeans	Denim fabric processed in cloud or sliver form, sometimes blended with cotton.	Can be used like cotton or blended.

Matching Preparation with Fiber

The way a fiber is prepared for spinning is as important as what kind of fiber it is. It may not have mattered when you were first trying to make yarn, when all you cared about was keeping the thread reasonably even and unbroken. But when you progress to trying to make a certain type of yarn—especially if matching a handspun and commercial yarn within the same project—the method of fiber preparation becomes important. In order to get a particular yarn, you may, for example, need a woolen preparation spun with a woolen draw, and worsted just won't do.

Knowing what type of fiber you have will help you know what type of yarn you can make. Worsted yarns, traditionally made from combed top, are best for hard-wearing garments like socks and mittens. They tend to pill less, are less fuzzy, and last longer than woolen yarns. Woolen yarns, made from airy carded preparations, trap a lot of air between the fibers, making them great insulators. Woolen yarns make warm hats and sweaters. They tend to pill more and wear out faster, so they're best used for garments that won't get hard wear.

To spin a woolen yarn, choose carded fibers, which include rolags, batts, and roving. You can make rolags with handcards or make batts using a drumcarder; roving and sliver are typically commercially produced preparations.

To spin a worsted yarn, use combed top. Although most of the handpainted fibers available (especially from small, independent dye companies) are

Cables and textured stitches are better defined in three-ply worsted-spun yarn (left) and are softer in woolen-spun singles (right).

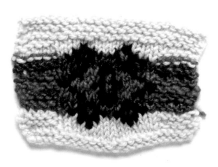

Colorwork is crisper in three-ply worsted-spun yarn (left) and is more blended in woolen-spun singles (right).

labeled as roving, a lot of them are really top. Unless you have a set of English combs, you are not unlikely to be able produce a true combed top, in which all the fibers are the same length and aligned parallel to each other.

Think about the type of fabric you want to make. When knitting stranded colorwork and cables, it's especially good to know your woolens from your worsteds. Do you want soft cables or defined cables? Soft cables come from woolen yarns, while defined ones are from worsted yarns.

Do you want your colorwork to have a watercolor effect, or do you want strong, defined lines? Woolen yarns will create softer, more blended colors, while defined, strong lines come from worsted yarns.

Roving or Top?

It can be difficult to tell top from roving just by looking at it—both present fibers in long tubes.

[1-2] To tell which is which, hold the fiber with your hands about a staple apart and pull.

[3] If the fiber separates in jagged, straggly wisps, it's roving.

[4] If the entire piece divides straight across, it's top.

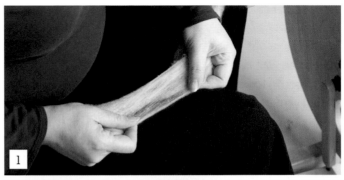
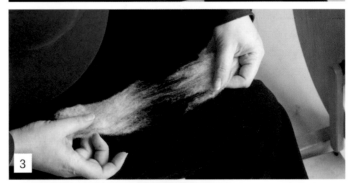

Is It Woolen or Worsted, and Why Should I Care?

Many spinners will contend that the only way to get a true woolen yarn is to use a fiber that was prepared in rolags, and the only true worsted yarn comes from fiber that was prepared with English combs. But between those two extremes are variations in preparation that will change—subtly or dramatically—the yarn that the fiber can become.

Preparations that use different lengths of fiber and arrange them in all directions by carding, such as rolags and batts, have woolen characteristics. The machines that produce roving and sliver align the fibers more, making these semiwoolen preparations. Preparations that remove all the fibers that aren't the same staple and arrange them as parallel as possible, such as combed top, are worsted preparations. Less aligned preparations that include different lengths of fibers are semiworsted.

In hand-combed top, the fibers are not only parallel, but the orientation of the fibers is preserved; all the tip ends face in one direction and all the cut ends in the other. Commercial top doesn't preserve that orientation, so some people consider it to be only semiworsted; I consider it a worsted preparation. The commercial process presses the fiber and subdues some

of the crimp, which makes the fibers lie more parallel. If top is wetted—as for hand-dyeing—some of the crimp becomes reactivated, and the fibers can float a bit out of alignment. For this reason, hand-dyed top has more semiworsted traits.

Spinning techniques, fibers, and fiber preparations have evolved together, so some fibers tend to be carded and spun with a long draw to create woolen yarns, while others are generally

combed and spun with a short forward draw to create worsted yarns. (See pages 32–35 for information on special spinning techniques for specific fiber preparations and pages 44–47 for woolen and worsted drafting methods.) But while it's helpful to know which techniques and preparations generally go together, you can match woolen techniques with worsted preparations and woolen preparations with worsted techniques. The yarns will have some of the traits of each.

The following rules of thumb help describe the yarn you make with a combination of techniques and fiber preparations.

Woolen preparation + woolen draw = woolen yarn

Woolen preparation + worsted draw = semiwoolen yarn

Worsted preparation + woolen draw = semiworsted yarn

Worsted preparation + worsted draw = worsted yarn

Any yarn that starts with a semiwoolen or semiworsted processed fiber will also be semiwoolen or semiworsted. If you aren't following all the requirements to make a purely worsted or woolen yarn, then a "semi" something is what you will produce. In my opinion, it doesn't matter much whether it's considered semiwoolen or semiworsted; it's "semi" and therefore neither fully woolen or worsted. Semiwoolen yarns are airier and fluffier than their semiworsted counterparts, but there is not as much difference between the two as between true woolen and worsted yarns.

You can still get gorgeous yarns no matter what combination of woolen and worsted properties they have. Sample different drafting methods and fibers to create just the yarn you want, and you'll be happy no matter what it's called. (See page 58 for more information on sampling.)

The Spectrum of Fiber Preparations

Between woolen rolags and worsted top is a wide range of fiber preparations. These common forms are just a portion of the ways fiber can be processed for spinning the whole range of yarns.

{woolen}

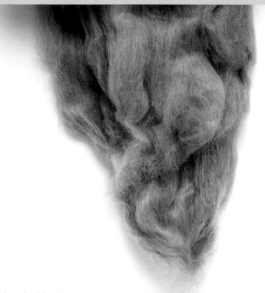

Blended batt

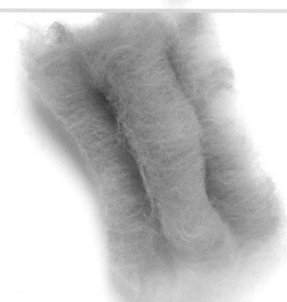

Handcarded rolags

{semiwoolen}

Hand-dyed pencil roving

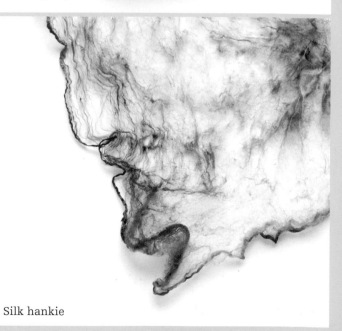

Silk hankie

{semiworsted}

{worsted}

Handpainted wool top

Hand-combed top

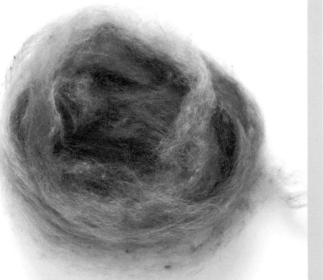

Silk hankie (attenuated)

Commercial top

Predrafting

When you were first learning to spin, you might have learned to predraft the fiber by stretching it out or splitting it lengthwise into a smaller diameter to make it easier to spin. If you're new to spinning, predrafting may help you, but don't do it so much that you aren't drafting at all while spinning. Well-prepared fiber doesn't *need* to be predrafted. Predrafting extensively can give you muddy colors in handpainted space-dyed fibers, and it can also lead to denser yarns if you have predrafted to the point that you aren't drafting at the wheel. Once you have practiced enough to manage both the fiber and twist when drafting, the main reasons to predraft are to make a difficult fiber easier to handle or to get a particular color variation.

Color is one of the key reasons to choose one method of predrafting over another. Do you want long color sections, short color sections, or something in between? Each technique will produce different results. Depending on the type of fiber preparation and the effect you're after, there are a few things to consider before predrafting.

Long color sections are produced with no predrafting or just a bit of fluffing. For a different distribution of color, you can strip top down to pieces about the diameter of your index finger. This breaks the color sections into short lengths, creating lovely variegation in your final yarn.

These aren't the only ways to predraft to manipulate the color. You could strip the top into more or fewer sections, or make a two-ply yarn from one stripped singles and one unstripped singles. Play with different methods of predrafting and make your own set of swatches to see what you like best.

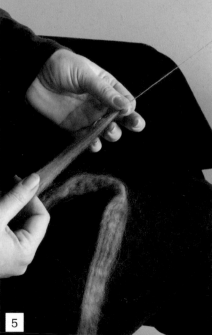

Alternatives to Predrafting

[1] Combed top in shades of red, purple, and yellow.

[2] Fluffing or opening up the top from side to side makes it easier to spin without interrupting the alignment of the top.

[3] Spinning the top with a short-draw technique (see page 44) and moving back and forth across the end of the fibers creates long sections of color.

[4–5] You can split the top almost as thin as you want your yarn to be, but no thinner. Spinning stripped sections of top creates short bursts of color in the yarn.

Effects of Predrafting in Color

This wool top was hand-dyed in three colors to show the variations in predrafting and the effects on your yarn. Each set includes a thick-and-thin low-twist singles, a two-ply yarn, and a Navajo- (or chain-) ply yarn. (See page 76 for two-ply yarns and page 92 for chain plying.)

Predrafted singles

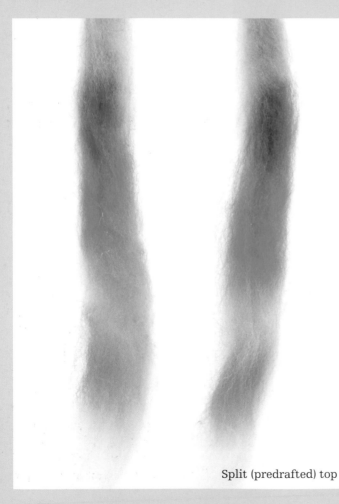

Split (predrafted) top

Singles without predrafting

Predrafted singles

Two-ply with one predrafted ply

Chain-ply without predrafting

Two-ply without predrafting

Chain-ply without predrafting

Predrafted two-ply

Predrafted chain-ply

Special Techniques for Specific Preparations

Certain fiber preparations call for special treatment when you sit down to spin. They can help you manage the fiber for successful spinning. (We'll cover a range of drafting techniques on pages 44–47.)

Top

Top may be compacted when it reaches you, either from being compressed in shipping or from hand-dyeing. Spinning compacted top can be excruciating. To make it easier to work with, you can fluff or open it sideways (see page 29) or pull off a length and swing it around in the air to loosen it.

If the fiber isn't tightly compacted, you can skip the fluffing—simply pull off a length in a size that is easy to manage and spin from that. Top is traditionally spun by moving the drafting zone across the fiber.

Roving and Sliver

You can spin roving and sliver without predrafting unless it is compacted— and I forego roving that is not fluffy and easy to spin. I'm pretty picky about my fiber in general; it should be airy enough for a spinner to grab a hunk and start spinning right away. You can predraft little "nests" of fiber for certain color variations, but for natural or solid-colored fibers, I generally break off a bit and spin as it is.

Batts

Batts are big sheets of fiber. Although you can spin from the end or side of the whole thing, you will probably want to separate it into smaller sections for easy handling. There are a few ways to handle a batt.

With a well-blended batt, any of these methods can produce an even yarn that doesn't change much in color variation. With a layered or incompletely blended batt, each method will produce different results because different portions of the batt may end up in different sections of the yarn. Which method you choose is all about the type of yarn you want and how comfortable you are with each method. (My personal favorite is the rolag method.)

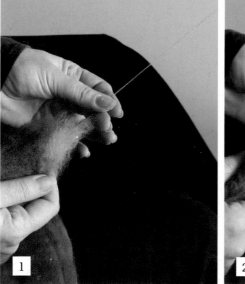

Spinning Top

[1] With practice, it's easy to spin yarn of any size from a piece of undrafted top.

[2] When spinning top, the drafting zone moves across the fiber.

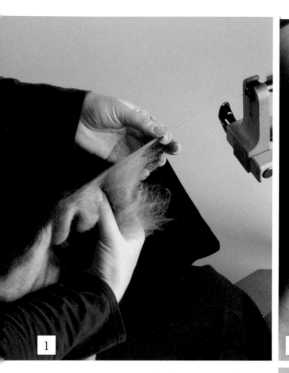

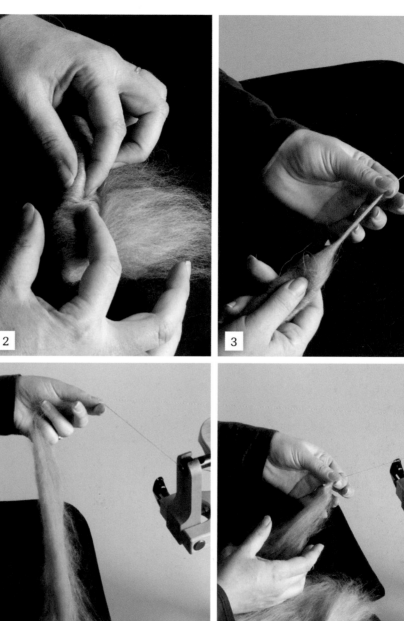

Options for Spinning Batts

[1] Open up the batt into a rectangle and spin from the end.

[2–3] Divide the batt lengthwise into short sections, roll them lengthwise like rolags, and spin from the end.

[4–5] Strip the batt from side to side (as for top) and spin from the end.

[6] Pull off a hunk and spin either from the fold or from the end of the piece.

Fleece

Fleece is wool as it was shorn off the sheep but not yet prepared for spinning. You can spin it as is, either after washing it (called *scouring*) or unwashed (called *in the grease*). In the grease is still full of lanolin that will coat your hands and wheel. Your hands will come away much softer for it. Nonetheless, I prefer to spin scoured fleece because I am not partial to the greasy, sticky feeling of the raw fleece. I find a washed fleece much easier to draft, and it doesn't leave lanolin on me or on my flyer and bobbins. Washed fleece can be processed by combing or carding (at home or in a mill).

For a different effect, you can spin from the lock (washed or not). Pull individual locks from the whole fleece. With your hands or a *flicker* (or flick carder), open up the ends so they're not clumped together. Then spin the lock from the tip end or from over the fold (see page 45).

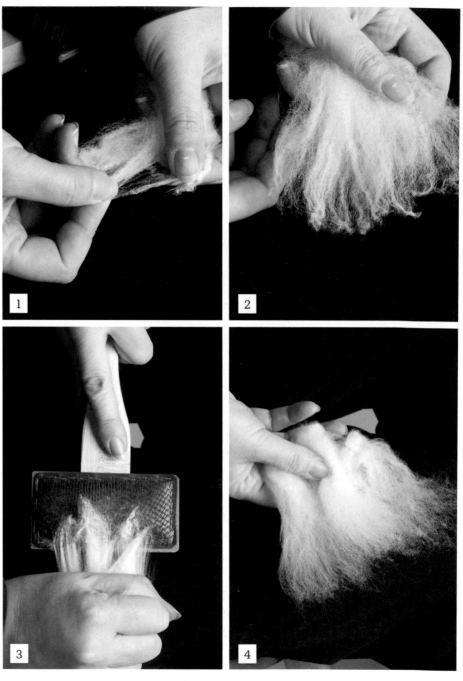

[1–2] Use your fingers to open up the ends of a lock.

[3–4] A flicker can open the ends of the fleece and remove dirt or chaff.

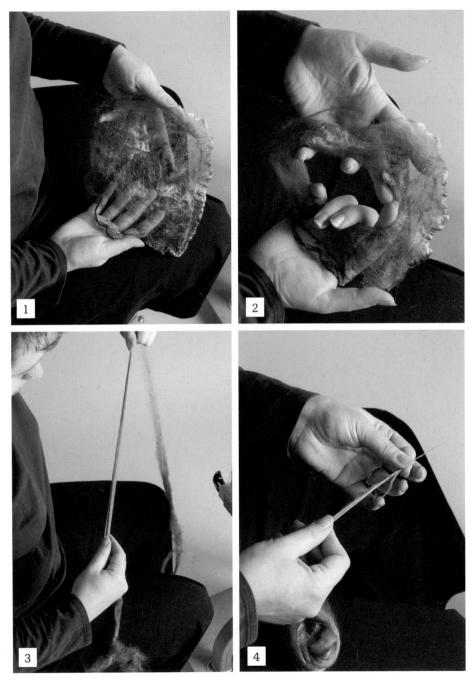

Silk Hankies

Silk is created in one long strand wrapped into a cocoon shape. When a cocoon is opened up instead of raveled or *reeled*, the fiber can be stretched over a form and made into a hankie, cap, or bell. This preparation makes it similar to carded wool in that all the strands are not going in the same direction.

Silk hankies are sold in stacks of many stretched cocoons. Tease the edges of the stack until you can pull off a single hankie. You should be able to see through it; each hankie is quite thin. Put one hand through the center of the hankie and start to pull it open into an oval. Keep slowly stretching it into a larger and larger oval. When you finally break the oval, you will have what looks like roving. You can predraft further or spin right from this. Predrafting will help you produce a thinner and more even yarn; the individual strands of silk are so long and strong that it can be difficult to draft them while spinning.

[1] Peel a single layer of silk from the stack. [2] Make a hole in the center and stretch it wide. [3] Draft the fiber to the desired thickness. [4] Wind the fiber into a nest and spin.

work with your wheel

There are more kinds of spinning wheels than most of us can imagine—from smaller than a carry-on bag to larger than a sofa. Whether you have borrowed a wheel, bought the wheel of your dreams, or own a whole collection, each one has unique traits that make it special and useful in its own way once you are familiar with it.

A spinning wheel is your partner in making yarn. While your hands draft and your feet treadle, the wheel adds the twist needed to turn loose fiber into cohesive yarn. This chapter will help you adjust your wheel and use your hands together to make the yarn you desire.

Make Friends with Your Wheel

Before you can get down to the fun of spinning on a wheel, it's important to get comfortable with it—find a comfortable position, learn to adjust it, and see what it's capable of. No matter what type of wheel you have, there are a few things that will help you get along well together.

Spinning in Comfort

One of the most important things for making friends with your wheel is how you relate to it physically. You may think a particular wheel just doesn't fit you or that it doesn't work right, but it may be how you sit in relation to the wheel that isn't working.

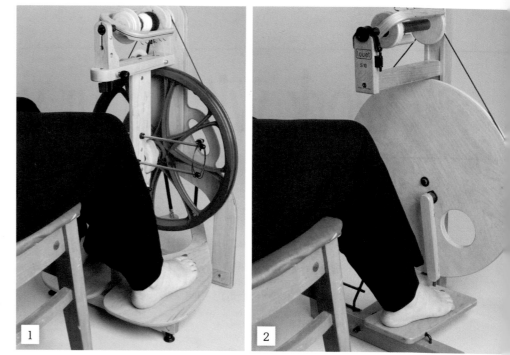

Spinning Posture

[1–2] Sit at a comfortable distance from the wheel.

[3–4] Don't sit too close to the wheel.

[5] Place your feet in a comfortable position on the treadle(s).

Your posture is more important to how you fit with your wheel than you may think. Most spinners can be comfortable spinning on any wheel if they sit in the correct position.

Start with a good stable seat. Rocking chairs, gliders, or other unstable seats are not good places to sit when spinning. Even if they're the right height, you will be working too hard to keep your body from moving to be effective at making yarn.

Sit facing the wheel at a height that ensures you aren't hunched over and your feet reach the treadle(s) comfortably. You may need to try out a couple of different chairs before you find the one that works with your body and your wheel. Sit at a comfortable distance from the wheel and adjust the distance so your whole leg doesn't do the treadling; your ankle should do all the work. If you use your whole leg, it can create leg pain or backaches. Sitting too close to the wheel—with your knees bent at

a 90-degree angle—will put you in an odd position and will make spinning for any length of time uncomfortable. If your feet are directly below your knees, move back a little bit.

Move your feet around on the treadle(s) if you don't immediately find a good spot. For a particular wheel, you might find that your feet need to be near the top, near the bottom, or smack-dab in the middle of the treadle. The only wrong foot placement on a treadle is the one

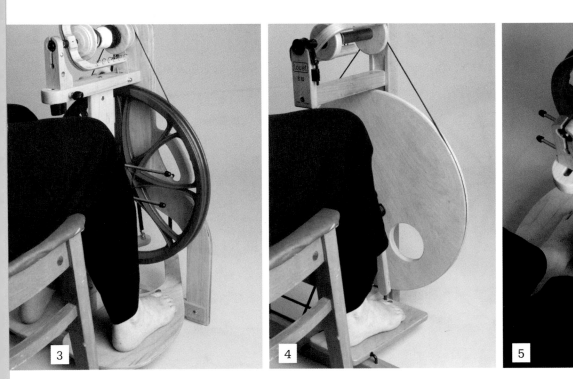

that makes you hurt or makes it hard to treadle. You should never feel as though you are treadling through molasses.

You will need to do this with any wheel that you own, try, or borrow. Sometimes you will find the sweet spot the second you sit down, while other times you may need to work at adjusting the chair or your position in relation to the wheel. Not finding the sweet spot immediately doesn't mean a particular wheel isn't the right wheel for you; sometimes the best things in life are the ones we have to work for.

Types of Wheels

From antique Sleeping Beauty-style Saxony wheels to ultra-modern upright wheels made from space-age materials, most spinning wheels in use today have a bobbin-and-flyer assembly. No matter how the parts are configured, spinning wheels work in similar ways to add twist and store your yarn.

Double-drive Wheels

Double-drive wheels use a single long drive band that turns both the bobbin and the flyer. In order for the yarn to be pulled onto the bobbin, there must be a difference in diameter between the groove on the bobbin and the groove of the whorl. The tension is adjusted by moving the entire mother-of-all, tightening or loosening the drive band. Many double-drive wheels can be converted to single-drive. Double-drive wheels are great for spinning very fine yarns, although they are capable of producing a wide range of yarns.

Single-drive Wheels

On single-drive wheels, there is one drive band and one brake band. On irish-tension (bobbin-lead) wheels, the drive band turns the bobbin and the brake band slows the flyer. Bobbin-lead wheels are excellent for spinning bulky yarns, though they can also create fine and medium yarns. On scotch-tension (flyer-lead) wheels, the drive band turns the flyer and the brake band slows the bobbin. Flyer-lead wheels are wonderful for spinning a wide variety of yarns.

Putting Your Wheel through the Paces

Are you familiar with your wheel? I mean *really* familiar. If you have it on its lowest ratio with the tension tight, what result will you have? Here's an exercise to help you really know your wheel.

Get several hundred yards of scrap yarn and prepare to feed it into your wheel as if you were making yarn. Use the smallest whorl you have and take off all the tension. Start treadling as if to make yarn. Feed in a few yards, then change the tension a little bit. For wheels with scotch or irish tensioning, increase the tension by turning the knob just one-eighth to one-fourth of a turn. For a double-drive wheel, start with the tensioning low so the drive band has slack in it but will still drive the flyer and bobbin. Adjust the tension on the drive band one-half turn, then feed the yarn on a bit more. Repeat until you've got the tension quite tight. Do this for each of the whorls on your wheel. *Do not* change the speed of your treadling—let the wheel do the work for you.

While you are doing this exercise, take mental notes (or, better yet, written ones) to remember how it all works. What happens with each whorl?

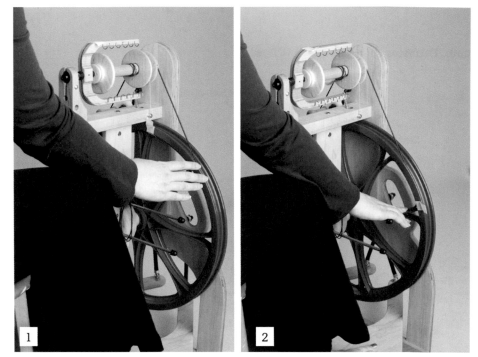

What's the Ratio?

[1] Mark a starting place on the flyer and wheel with a piece of tape.

[2] Count the number of times the flyer goes around per full turn of the drive wheel.

How about at each tension level? Understanding what happens when you adjust your wheel is key to knowing what your wheel can do and how it can help you achieve the results you want. It may seem tedious now, but it's less painful to know the settings of your wheel than to waste time (and fiber!) trying to figure it out before each new project. Being familiar with your wheel will mean you can get right to spinning in the future.

Understanding Ratios and Wheel Adjustments

The ratios on a spinning wheel mean that for every time the drive wheel turns once, the flyer or bobbin will turn a given number of times. For example, a ratio of 9:1 means that every time the drive wheel turns once, the flyer or bobbin goes around 9 times. The diameter of the whorl determines how fast the bobbin or flyer will turn in relation to the drive wheel; every groove on the whorl produces a different ratio.

While treadling at the same speed, you can make a fat yarn or a thin yarn by choosing a different ratio (assuming your wheel has a range of available ratios). A wheel set at a 6:1 ratio (a larger whorl) will be slow and put less twist into the yarn, which is perfect for making a bulky yarn. The same wheel set at a ratio of 18½:1 (a smaller whorl) will put more twist into the yarn, so that while treadling at the same speed as for the fat yarn, you can make a thin high-twist yarn.

Some wheels are capable of a wide range of ratios while others are set up to make a specific type of yarn. When you can, use the right wheel for the job. For example, Country Bulky spinners are great for making thick low-twist yarns; most of them have lovely slow ratios. Using one of those to make a high-twist yarn will be quite a bit of work. I'm not going to tell you that you can't (because someone will do it to prove to me that it can be done), but just because it can be done doesn't mean it's the best route to take. (See page 80 for a few tricks to make finer yarns without changing the ratio.) The same goes for using a wheel for which the lowest ratio is 18½:1—it's not the most efficient way to make low-twist bulky yarn. Knowing

what your wheel can (and cannot) do well will help prevent headaches in the future.

As I describe how to make certain yarns, I won't ask you to set the wheel at a certain ratio. There are so many wheels and different ratios that I couldn't give you a specific one; you may not even have the one I'd use. With a few exceptions, most wheels can make most yarns, and you will learn to make most yarns no matter what wheel you have. The previous exercise will have shown you how best to use your wheel.

Wheel Maintenance

Set a time to clean your wheel! Clean off any fiber and gunk from moving parts so it's sparkling, then add new oil. This will help your wheel live a long life. I clean after every 2 pounds of fiber or if I have let the wheel sit for any length of time.

Some wheels are naturally oil-hungry. If oil isn't working to keep your wheel from squeaking, try using a bit of beeswax, especially where wood meets metal. For leather parts, use saddle conditioner (found in any tack shop) to keep the leather from getting brittle.

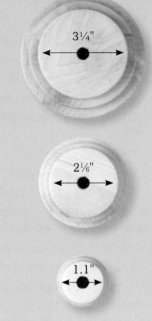

Whorls and Ratios

3¼"

2⅙"

1.1"

The smaller groove of the slow-speed whorl (top) turns the flyer 6 times each time the 19½" drive wheel turns once. The medium-speed whorl (middle) turns 9 times, and the super-high-speed whorl (bottom) turns 18½ times.

My favorite drive band for double-drive wheels is mercerized cotton. My wheels have some colorful bands left over from knitting projects. A mercerized cotton band stretches before the first bobbin is finished, so cut and reknot it after the first time you use it. The band usually doesn't stretch again until about 20 pounds of fiber have been spun. If your cotton drive band is slipping too much, try running it through some natural beeswax.

The Long and Short of the Draw

Once you understand the abilities and nuances of your wheel, it's time for the fun part—time to make yarn! While the wheel is making twist, your hands are busy controlling how that twist meets the fibers.

There are many methods to create yarn. You could start and end a project with similar products but use a million different methods to get there. I won't tell you that any method you are using is wrong; handspun is a beautiful thing, and as long as you are happy with your product, keep doing it! However, if you are having a hard time making the yarn you want, it may be your technique. If you need to make a certain yarn and it's not working out, it may be helpful for you to learn how to spin with a few different traditional methods.

The way you draft out the fibers makes all the difference in the yarn you produce. Along with fiber, choosing a drafting method is the most important decision in planning your spinning project.

Short Draw

[1–2] In short forward draw, the front hand moves back and forth, keeping twist out of the drafting triangle.

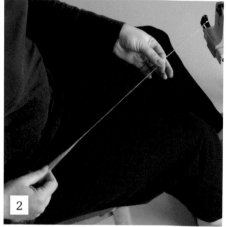

Long Draw

[1–2] In long draw, the back hand pulls the fiber back against the twist and the front hand makes minor adjustments.

Short Draw or Inchworm

Short draw is a method for spinning worsted yarns. One hand remains stable while the other hand drafts; the front hand helps slick down the fibers to make a sturdy yarn and keeps twist out of the drafting triangle. Short draw is

about keeping your hands close to one another. This is generally considered the easiest method for beginners to start with. For many spinners, it is the position that their hands automatically go to when sitting down with fiber.

Long Draw

Long draw is a method for making woolen yarns. There are many variations on long draw, but all involve twist in the drafting zone. One hand does most of the work, moving back and forth to draw the fiber out and then letting it go into the orifice. The other hand may make minor adjustments and control when the twist enters the fibers. This method allows twist in the drafting triangle, where it plays a role in drafting the fiber.

Fiber preparation is more important for long draw than for any other method. Long draw is best done using a carded airy fiber, traditionally rolags, so that it is easy to draft out the fiber smoothly. If the fiber is too dense or clumpy, it will translate into an uneven yarn.

This method is easiest for most spinners when the wheel is set to produce high twist (fast ratio) and moderate take-up (tension). It requires some faith that your fiber won't break before enough twist enters to stabilize it. You may need quite a bit of practice, but once you master it, you'll feel like you've won a marathon.

Spinning from the Fold

This is my favorite method for working with slippery fibers. Break off an easy-to-handle piece of fiber—for me, that's about 4 inches long and 2 inches wide. Fold it over the index finger of your forward hand. Grasp the hanging ends with your thumb and other fingers but don't put a strangle hold on them.

Tease out a bit of fiber from the tip of your index finger. Attach that little bit to your leader as you would for any

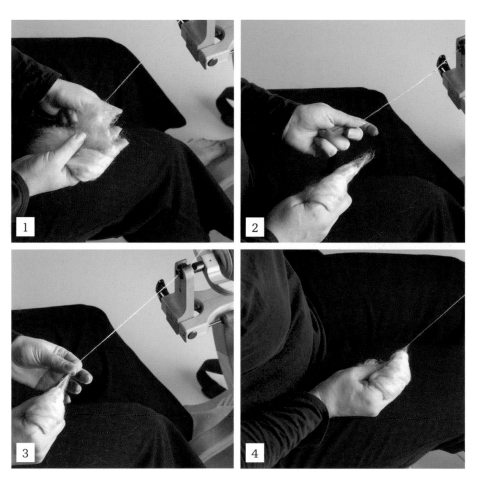

method of spinning. Draft the fiber from the tip of the finger, keeping a loose hold on the remaining fibers in your hand. As you finish one bunch of fiber, start another in the same manner.

Spinning from the fold bends the fibers in half, making a springy yarn, and gives you more control over long fibers that can be hard to draft. It can be used with a short draw to make a worsted-style yarn or with a long draw to make a woolen-style yarn.

Spinning from the Fold

[1] Fold a length of fiber over your index finger.

[2] Attach the leader to the tip of the teased-out fiber.

[3] Use a short forward draw to make semiworsted yarn.

[4] Use a long backward draw to make semiwoolen yarn.

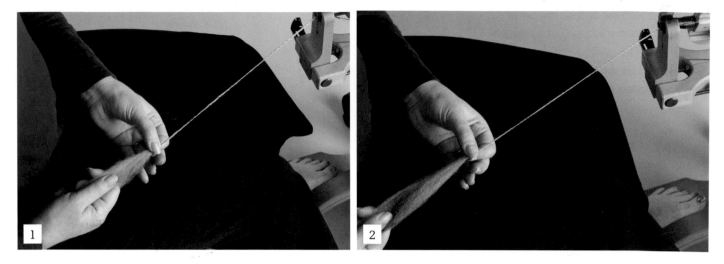

Modified Long Draws

There are many methods that could be described as modified long draw but could also be considered regular long draw. It's hard to define; some schools of thought hold that any of these modified methods are worsted spinning, while others allow that some may be considered woolen. The long draw that works best with a double-drive wheel is a *supported long draw*, in which twist is allowed into the fiber and the front hand holds the fiber, creating tension for the back hand to pull against. On a wheel with scotch or irish tension, this tension is already present, but it's necessary to create it manually with a double-drive wheel. In my opinion, this method is woolen spinning while the next two methods are more worsted types.

American long draw has the back hand holding the fiber loosely while the front hand drafts the fiber out. Here, too, twist goes into the fiber supply as the fiber is drafted.

Sliding long draw may be the most typical of all modified long draws; the hand movements are similar to those in short draw except that there is a longer drafting length.

Double Draw

Double draw (or double drafting) is typically used with "cloud-prepared" fibers, which are short fibers that have been cleaned and opened but not carded into roving or batts. These include very soft luxurious fibers like bison, yak, and other types of down. These fibers are so short that you may have a hard time drafting out in other ways; double drafting makes them surprisingly strong.

Sliding Long Draw

[1–2] Spinning with a long draw and smoothing down the fibers is a modified long-draw technique.

Treadle the wheel to build up some twist in your leader, lay a bit of the fiber over the leader, and let the twist go into a long length of it as you draw back your fiber hand. When you have a few feet of lumpy, uneven yarn between your hands, stop drafting out; it will be weak in some areas. Using both hands, go back over the fibers to smooth and draft out the rough spots. Keep treadling and adding twist as you go. When the yarn is more even and has enough twist to hold together, feed it onto the bobbin and begin again.

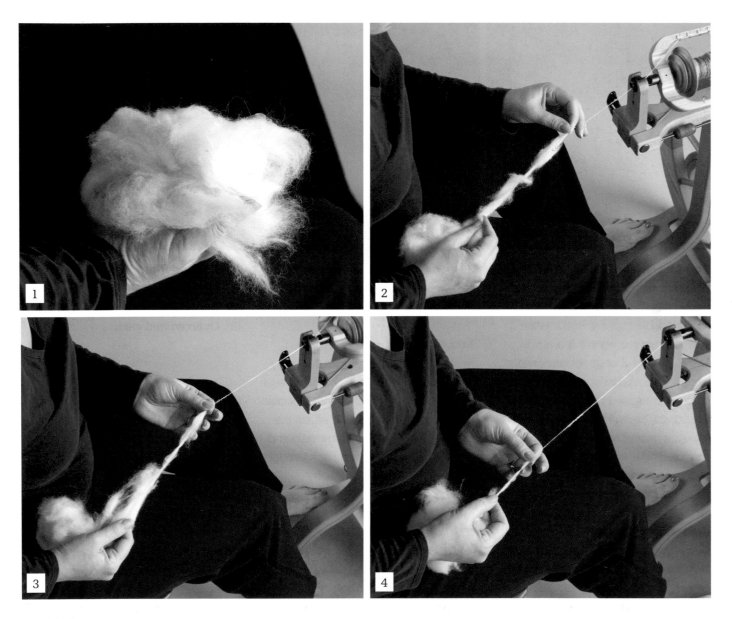

Double Draw

[1] Double drafting is often used for short, fluffy fibers prepared like a cloud.

[2] Pull out a length of lumpy, uneven yarn.

[3] Smooth and draft the uneven places in the yarn.

[4] The resulting yarn is surprisingly smooth and durable.

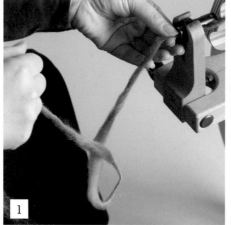

Too Little, Too Much, Just Right

While spinning, check to be sure that the singles you're making have the right amount of twist to become the finished yarn you want. For a quick check, pull out a length of freshly spun yarn. Low-twist yarn doesn't twist back on itself; energized yarn (as for plying) twists back on itself; overtwisted yarn makes a gnarly mess if given the chance. This is known as the plyback test, because you're examining how the yarn might look when plied with itself.

Correcting Twist

If you have a bobbin of yarn with more twist than you'd like, place the bobbin on your lazy kate as if to ply (except that you are using only one bobbin) and attach the yarn to the leader on an empty bobbin on the wheel. With a low ratio and fast draw-in, run the yarn back through the wheel in the direction *opposite* to which it was made. (If you spun

Z singles, turn the wheel to spin S). This will remove some twist—just be mindful not to remove too much.

If your yarn doesn't have enough twist, there are no rules that say you can't add more! (And if there were such a rule, we'd break it.) Set up the bobbin on the kate as if to ply and attach the yarn to the leader. With a low ratio and fast draw-in, run the yarn back through in the *same* direction in which it was made.

Plying: Whys and Wherefores

Unless you plan to use the yarn as singles (see page 66), plying is the next step after spinning. Depending on your perspective, plying can be fun or tedious, but plying well can make your yarn glorious. Plying creates a balanced yarn, but there are other good reasons to ply. It makes yarn

Finding the Right Twist

[1] Low-twist yarn

[2] Energized yarn

[3] Overtwisted yarn

thicker, stronger, and less likely to pill. You can create more color and texture effects when you ply. Anyone can ply yarns together; plying well is the trick. There are a few simple rules and techniques that can help you ply better and get beyond the basics.

Working on a big project? Spin all your singles before you ply. Your yarn often changes from your first bobbin to the last. It happens to the best of us, but the note-card trick (see page 59) will help reduce variation in the yarn. To keep your yarn more even throughout, ply bobbins in an order different from the order in which they were spun.

For example, if you have 6 bobbins of yarn arranged in order of spinning, ply number 1 with 6, 2 with 5, and 3 with 4.

When plying, make sure that your hands are keeping all the strands of yarn under equal tension. If one yarn is held more taut than the other, the loose one will spin around the tight one. This is the basis for some excellent novelty techniques but not so good if you are aiming for a nice, even two-ply yarn. It's best to hold the yarn in a way that keeps one finger between the plies. It will help you maintain even tension.

Plying Twist

How much twist do you need to add while plying? The right amount of plying twist depends on the amount of spinning twist.

Measuring the twist in the yarn as you go can seem tedious, especially for those who aren't as interested in the technical aspects of spinning. (See page 63 for information on measuring twist.) Instead of getting out a ruler, a good test is to pull out a foot or two of plied yarn and let it go slack. This is similar to the plyback test, which you may use when spinning singles to make sure that they have the right amount of twist for the finished yarn (see page 63). An overtwisted yarn will kink up on itself, while a balanced two-ply yarn should hang limp or barely cross itself. While this method isn't perfect, it can give you a good indication of whether the singles you're spinning will have enough twist for the yarn you're planning.

I often add a little extra twist to my yarn when plying because some of the singles twist will be dormant and some of the ply twist will relax during finishing. I also make a lot of overplied yarns because I prefer the added strength from more twist for garments like mittens and socks that take a beating.

It may seem as if the ultimate goal is a "balanced" yarn, but there is no rule that you have to make it that way. Underplied yarns aren't always fun to work with, but the handspinning police will not come and remove your wheel should you make one. You're the one using the yarn, and you're the one who needs to be happy with it.

If you don't like the plying you've just done, you can add more twist by running the yarn through the wheel again in the plying direction (usually S). If you think it's too twisty, run it through the wheel again in the direction opposite the plying direction (Z).

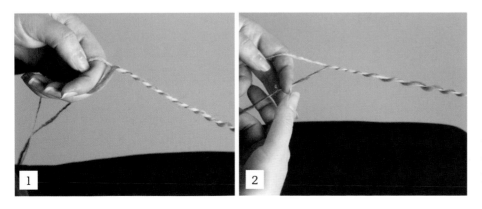

Plying Twist
[1] Keep a finger between the singles as you ply to help maintain even tension.

[2] Holding the singles under uneven tension will make one yarn wrap around the other instead of plying evenly.

The Lazy Kate

A lazy kate is a crucial tool for plying. There are many views on what type of lazy kate is best and where the kate should be positioned with respect to the spinner. Should the kate be tensioned? Should it sit in front of you, to the side, or behind you?

You may have noticed that the singles tend to kink up if there is no tension on the kate. If you yank the yarn off the bobbins and then feed it into the wheel, you probably know all about the tangling problem. One way to solve this is with a tensioned kate, but simply keeping the yarn moving steadily with even tension will prevent the yarn from twisting on itself.

Where the kate is positioned makes a big difference, too. Kates that are attached to the wheel work in a pinch and are handy if you're traveling, but they are prone to trouble from the "yank and feed" method. Just becoming aware of it may help you avoid the problem. If you're having difficulty and don't have a kate at hand, make one out of knitting needles and a shoe box or plastic crate. Set the kate behind and to the side of you as you ply. Pulling the singles forward from this position is a more natural motion. All the yarn is moving forward into the wheel, and it's easier to keep a steady motion.

Fresh Yarn

If you've been spinning two (or more) bobbins of singles for plying, chances are that some of the singles are more freshly spun than others. Yarn on the bobbin starts to relax immediately. This doesn't mean that it untwists; it means that some of the energy relaxes or goes dormant. If you have one bobbin of yarn that is several days old and try to ply it with a freshly spun yarn, one will have relaxed quite a bit, while the twist in the other is fresh and active. It's not impossible to ply fresh and older yarns together, but it will be easier to gauge the right amount of twist needed if both yarns are equally fresh.

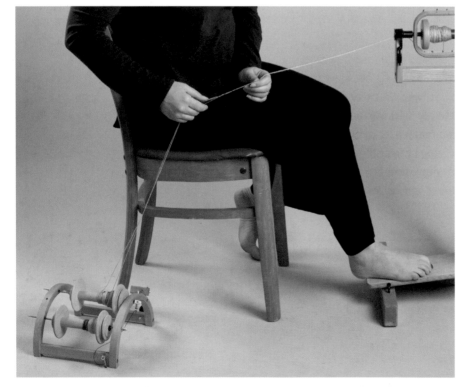

Positioning the kate behind and to the side of you will help you draft the singles smoothly.

Correcting Errors While Plying

If you have a little slub that sneaked through when you were spinning singles, you can take care of it when you ply. Let the ply run over it, then grasp it and yank. It usually comes free without leaving a trace.

It's good to know how to splice for those times when yarn breaks during plying or when one bobbin empties and you need to add another. To make a join, keep the plying twist out of the drafting triangle and overlap the broken ends of yarn by a few inches. Twist them together, then gently allow the plying twist to come in and lock the ends in place.

Even with these rules of thumb, some spinners may have difficulty getting the plied yarn they want. Plying takes practice and understanding of the principles behind it. Pretty soon you'll have that "Aha!" moment, and you'll want to holler from a mountain peak that you did indeed make the perfect plied yarn.

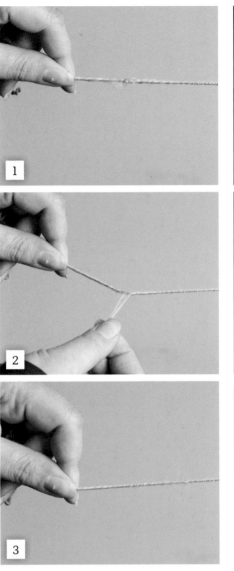

Fixing Slubs

[1] You may be able to fix a slub in your singles while plying.

[2] Grab the slub and tug it gently.

[3] The slub will usually disappear from the yarn.

Splicing

[1] If a strand breaks or you need to add a new bobbin, it's time to splice.

[2] Overlap the broken ends and twist them together.

[3] The plying twist will secure the join.

measuring success

To *improve your spinning,* it might seem like all you need to do is spend more time at the wheel. (Go on, twist my arm.) While practice makes perfect, there are a few things to do away from the wheel that can make your yarns come out closer to the ones in your dreams. From giving your freshly spun skein the perfect finish to keeping records that will help you spin even better yarn next time, this chapter will introduce you to a variety of techniques that can help you make great yarn every time.

Unfinished yarn

Finished yarn

Finishing Yarn

To finish or not to finish—that is the question. Finishing a yarn means setting the twist by washing. The specific technique depends on what fiber you're using and what effect you're after.

Some people swear by not finishing a yarn before using it, while others say it's barbaric not to finish a yarn. If you're planning to use energized singles, you don't want any twist to settle, which will remove some of the desired energy. It might be tempting to skip finishing because you want to start knitting sooner, but keep in mind that most fibers change character within a yarn from the unfinished to finished state. If you're going to plan and knit a whole project, it's worth spending the time to finish the yarn so that you don't have surprises when the whole piece is completed. Finished yarns can change yardage and gauge. Yarns tend to plump and fluff as they settle into their twist. You need to set the twist to get an accurate gauge. To finish any yarn, wind it into a hank using a skein winder, niddy-noddy, the back of a chair, or your elbow. Tie the hank securely but loosely in several places.

Animal Protein Yarns

To set the twist in yarns made from animal protein, fill a basin with warm, soapy water and soak the hank for 10 to 15 minutes (see page 55). Be careful not to agitate the yarn. Fill another basin with clean water of the same temperature.

Remove the hank from the soapy water and gently squeeze the water out without wringing. Submerge it in the basin with clean water and soak for another 5 to 10 minutes. Pull it out, squeeze out the water, and hang it to dry.

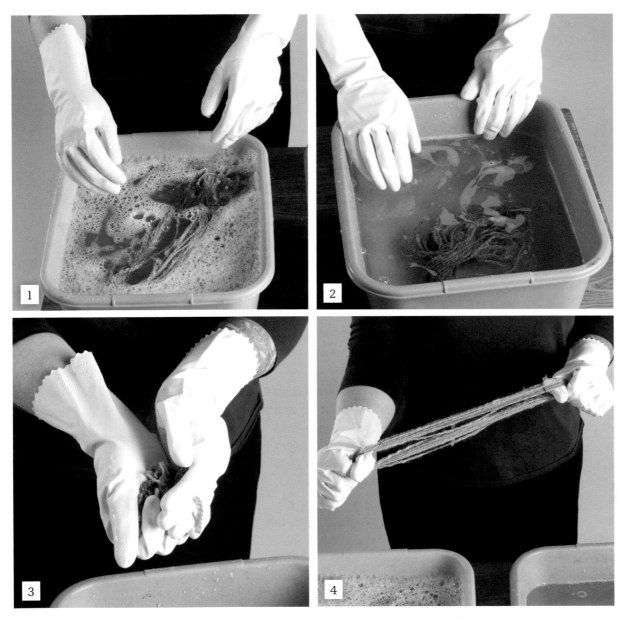

Standard Finishing for Animal Protein Yarns

[1–2] Soak the skein in warm, soapy water, then rinse.

[3–4] Squeeze the water out of the skein and snap or thwack it.

Cellulose Yarns

To set the twist in yarn made from bast or cotton fibers, put the hank of yarn in a large pot and cover it with enough water so that the fiber moves freely. Add about ¼ cup of washing soda and let the water boil for 30 minutes. Rinse the yarn in cool water. If bast fibers have left the water murky, repeat these steps until the water is clear. Wring out the excess water and hang to dry.

Silk and Synthetic Yarns

To set the twist on silks and synthetics, you can use the soak and hang method, but I prefer to set the twist with steam. This can be achieved in a steamer or by laying out the hank of yarn and applying steam by holding a steam iron 4 to 6 inches (10–15 cm) from the yarn. This is my chosen method because it plumps the yarn and keeps it vibrant; I find that silk given a hot-water bath will sometimes seem dull once it's dry.

Blended Yarns

For blended yarns, I use the method that corresponds with the major component in the blend. Of course, the method to set bast and cotton fibers is likely to full wool fiber, so use your judgment when choosing a method for setting the twist.

My favorite finishing method is to soak the hank in warm, soapy water, then soak it in cold water. Once I've wrung out the water by hand or in the spin cycle of the washing machine, I snap it between my hands or (if I have the luxury to be outside) smack it against a table. Not only does it help the yarn settle and even out the twist, it helps me work out a few frustrations. Refrain from whacking more than once or twice—beating the yarn excessively can sometimes felt it.

I never weight a skein of yarn when drying. It stretches out the individual fibers, removing all elasticity (especially in animal protein yarns). Once the yarn is wet again, the elasticity will return. If you had a kinky, twisty skein of yarn that was weighted while drying so that it would be easy to knit with, the kinkiness will return when the finished piece is washed, with less-than-desirable results. If you weight a yarn that was already balanced, it will remove any elasticity, and working with it may feel like working with straw. (When you are spinning for a warp, it may be to your advantage to have less elastic yarn.)

Fulling Finish

Although we're usually careful not to agitate wet, soapy yarn in case it felts, fulling yarn can give it strength and a different texture. Low-twist singles are often fulled for strength and durability (see page 72). This finish needs to be done with caution. You can do it in a washing machine, but I prefer the control of doing it by hand. The washing machine is fast, and the process can easily get out of control in a short amount of time.

Fill two basins with water, one with quite hot and soapy water and one with ice-cold water. Make sure your hank of yarn is tied in at least four places, preferably with yarn that won't felt. The yarn will take a beating, so the ties need to be secure—not tight, just secure. Wearing good kitchen gloves (the kind with texture on the palms is best), dunk the yarn in the hot, soapy water and rough it up—swoosh it around and rub it between your hands. You can also use a plunger to create more friction. Squeeze the water out of the hank and dunk it in the cold water. Pick it up, squeeze out the water, and do it all over again. I do this several times, until the strands of yarn are just starting to stick together. Keep an eye on your yarn and check it often. The yarn can be fulled a little or a lot; it's up to you how you want the yarn to look and behave. Give the yarn a thwack, whack, or snap and hang it to dry.

Fulling Yarn

[1–2] Soak the yarn in very hot water and agitate it.

[3–4] Dunk the skein in cold water and squeeze it out. Repeat the hot water, agitation, and cold water until the strands begin to stick together.

Sample

Sampling can be the difference between joy and disappointment at the end of a spinning project. When spinning for a project you've been dreaming of, try out the fiber and spinning methods you want to explore before you start spinning the whole project. Stop after spinning for a few minutes and test-drive the yarn before spinning up pounds of fiber. Ply a few yards and finish them the way you plan to finish the project, knit (or crochet or weave) a swatch, and see if the yarn does what you want. Try a few different techniques—spinning long draw or over the fold, three- or four-ply, fulling or standard finish—and see which of the yarns has the properties you're looking for.

This isn't just a good practice to fine-tune the specific project you have in mind, it's also an investment in all your future spinning projects. Sampling may seem to take too much time and waste energy and fiber, but it's actually a big time-saver in the long run.

If you make a bunch of samples before spinning, you'll have a better idea of what to do the next time you want to spin a similar yarn. Keep these samples handy; you may want to attach them to your spinning journal or make up cards

Gauge swatches of this yarn as a two- and three-ply helped decide which to use for my sweater.

to keep in a pocket near your wheel. A good sample card keeps singles and plied yarn (finished and unfinished) together, so that the next time you want to make the same yarn, you are able to reproduce it.

I was recently mooning over a certain sweater that I wanted to make in handspun. I wanted to use a Merino/silk 80/20 blend that I was familiar with, and I wanted to spin it from the fold. I made a two-ply and a three-ply to swatch for the sweater. Having worked with similar yarns before, I was fairly sure that one would be right. Both worked, but I found that the two-ply sample had a better drape in the pattern I chose. Sometimes you choose a yarn based on stitch definition, or gauge, or how the final fabric drapes. There are so many variables at play, and it's a great thing to be in charge of it all when you spin.

If I hadn't been familiar with the fiber or I wasn't sure how I wanted to spin it, I would have needed to make more yarn samples. I would have made some

yarn with a long draw and some short draw. And if neither two-ply nor the three-ply had been right for the project I had in mind, it would have been back to the drawing board and making more sample yarns.

All this means that you need more fiber. (That's right—show this to anyone who questions your buying habits. *You need more fiber.*) If you're buying fiber for a specific project, buy 4 ounces or more extra so that you can sample and be sure you know how to make the right yarn.

Once you have the right yarn figured out, attach samples of the finished and unfinished yarns to a card (often called a control card). Keep the card by your wheel and check your spinning against the sample card every so often. By matching your yarn to the sample, you will know that you are creating a reliable yarn for your project.

Keeping Records

What fiber did you use for the gorgeous piece you just finished knitting? Which wheel(s) did you use, and on what ratio? What drafting methods did you use? If you keep notes and samples of your spinning projects, you are on your way to writing your own reference notebook. Information on past spinning projects will help you with future yarns, especially if you want to duplicate something.

In addition to the technical information, I keep a sample of the unwashed singles, the unwashed plied yarn (if I plied), and the finished yarn. Since yarns often change quite a bit when you wash them, keeping the unwashed samples gives you something to match your new yarns to. The washed sample shows what the final outcome should be if using the same techniques and fiber content. You could record all the measurements like twists per inch and wraps per inch (see page 62), but I

prefer to keep samples of the yarn and gather the information from them when needed.

Keep this information in one place in your very own spinning journal. Make a gorgeous scrapbook with photos, yarn samples, and notes. It can be a small journal or a large one. Use a hole punch to attach lengths of yarn to the paper. It may seem tedious to keep all these notes when you'd rather play with your brand-new yarn or fiber, but when you refer to the journal you will be thrilled that you did this for yourself. Make one that you are happy with, and you'll use it more often.

This control card keeps samples of the singles, unfinished two-ply, and finished two-ply handy.

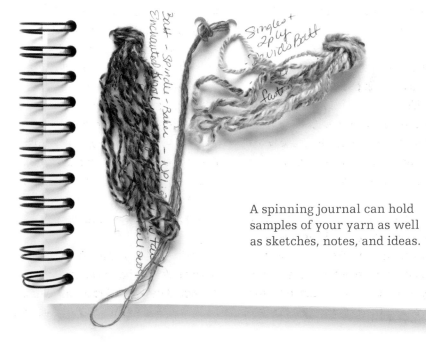

A spinning journal can hold samples of your yarn as well as sketches, notes, and ideas.

Analyzing Yarn

If you need a very specific yarn—if you need a handspun yarn to go with a millspun yarn or want to duplicate a handspun yarn—look no further than the yarn itself for major clues. Knitters, crocheters, weavers, and other crafters learn to "read" their work, to see where they've been and what comes next by looking at the fabric that's been made so far. It's the same with making the yarn itself: it's really helpful to see the characteristics of the yarn and know how it was made. (Don't forget to make notes and keep your samples. If you're good about keeping records, you will save yourself loads of time the next time you need to replicate yarn.)

What Is It Made Of?

Start by reading the tag, if there is one—what is the fiber composition? You may guess from the fuzzy halo that it contains some mohair, or a cool matte surface might suggest cotton, but blends can be deceiving. If there isn't a tag on the yarn, there are a few tests to help narrow down the possibilities. The burn test is a simple way to identify a general category of fiber. Use safety precautions like eye protection, keep a fire extinguisher nearby, and perform the test in a clean, well-ventilated space away from children and pets. Place a 4-inch (10 cm) piece of yarn in a heat-safe dish and light one end on fire. Observe how it looks, smells, smokes, and burns.

Can you tell at first glance how this yarn was constructed?

Vegetable fibers (including rayons) burn easily and smell like burning paper, leaves, or wood. They glow before the flame dies out and leave behind a fine gray ash. Animal fibers retreat from the flame and usually go out by themselves when the flame is removed, but they do burn. They smell like burning hair; some are quite strong, but silk has a more mellow odor. They leave behind a hollow black bead that's easily crushed. Synthetics melt, burn, and retreat from the flame. Most synthetics smell acrid and unnatural when burned. They generally leave behind a hard, solid black bead.

Figuring out the fiber type more precisely may take time and practice. And after trying to figure out what fibers are in your own yarn a few times, you may start to take really good notes!

How Many Plies?

You will probably be able to identify singles yarn right away, though some commercial yarns are actually made from two singles spun again in the same direction. Use your hands to untwist the end of the yarn a bit to see how many plies are there. Some interesting yarns are cabled; they take a more careful eye when unplying to discover the individual components, but you can do it. You probably won't be able to deconstruct chained or sewn yarns. These are not easy to duplicate, and you may need to make a complementary rather than matching yarn.

Worsted or Woolen?

This is hard to tell; you may not know for sure how the yarn was spun. In general, woolen yarns are fluffier and airier; they will have more yardage per pound than worsted yarns. Worsted yarns tend to have fewer flyaway fibers;

they are often tougher or denser. (There are only a few commercial woolen yarns available; they are usually from smaller mills.)

How Was It Finished?

You'll probably be able to tell if the yarn was fulled, but other than that you won't be able to identify a specific finishing method. Once you full a yarn of your own (and I recommend it, even if just for reference), you will be able to recognize it in commercial yarns.

How Thick Is Each Ply?

Many fibers will puff up when the twist is set. This means that when you are trying to emulate a yarn that has already been set, you need to test the fiber you are using to see how it expands before being able to spin the correct thickness. If you want to match a yarn in thickness and grist, make small samples and finish them to find the one that works the best.

Counting Plies

[1] Untwist the end of the yarn to see how many plies it is made from.

[2] Each of the plies in this yarn is made of three strands. It's a nine-strand cabled yarn, made from three Navajo- (or chain-) plied yarns.

Math and Measurements

As a beginning spinner, you may have avoided thinking about math as much as possible. After all, the enticing feeling of fiber running through your fingers and the beauty of a skein of yarn can't be summed up with numbers. But as you improve your spinning technique and practice making consistent yarns that meet your needs, a few mostly painless calculations and measurements will make the task easier.

Much of knowing the measurements of a yarn has to do with successfully duplicating your yarn. Sometimes you just want to spin, but at other times you've made the most perfect yarn you've ever spun, and you'll want to duplicate it. Spinning and hoping is one way; the other is keeping samples that you can measure later or making the measurements now. What are the twists per inch and the wraps per inch of both the singles and the plied yarn before finishing? Determining this is an accurate way of making sure you get the same yarn again.

If you finish the yarn and then take these measurements, you may be fooling yourself. Some fibers puff and fluff considerably with washing. This will mean that if you measure the twists per inch and the wraps per inch *after* finishing, you may end up with a very different yarn when you try to duplicate it based on those specifications.

Wraps Per Inch

The number of wraps per inch (wpi) indicates the grist or weight of the yarn. Wrap a strand of yarn around a ruler or wpi gauge, holding the yarn so that it doesn't kink but without stretching it. The wraps should be close enough to each other to cover the ruler or space but not so close that they crowd each other. Count the number of wraps per inch at several different places in your skein in case the diameter of the yarn changed as you were spinning.

In general, the fewer wraps per inch of yarn, the larger the needle, hook, or reed you will use to work with it. One quick trick for choosing needles or hooks is to double the yarn and pass it through the holes in a needle gauge or hook gauge to see which hole it fits through best. Start swatching with that size needle or hook, then decide whether the fabric should be tighter or looser.

Inserting the doubled-up yarn in a needle gauge can help you find the right needle size.

This yarn measures 14 wraps per inch (wpi).

If you don't know the wraps per inch of a yarn when you are ready to use it, you can still use the yarn, but it may take some guessing as far as the needle, hook, or reed you need to use. You might find yourself unhappy with the results if you don't do some sort of measuring. For knitting and crochet, you can, of course, use the needle/hook gauge method mentioned above. It doesn't work as well for weaving if you want a balanced weave.

Measuring Twist: Twists Per Inch and Twist Angle

The fundamentals of plying have to do with twists per inch (tpi). When plying, you start with singles that are overtwisted and balance the twist through the yarn. For example, take singles with 8 twists per inch. Plying two of these together requires 4 twists per inch to balance the resulting yarn. Singles with 12 twists per inch need to be plied at 6 twists per inch for a two-ply yarn. I often prefer to ply yarns a bit more tightly than these simple calculations would suggest, as some of that twist will relax when the yarn is washed. To use the first example of singles at 8 twists per inch, I would usually ply to 5 twists per inch, which will settle at about 4 twists per inch when washed. I prefer tough, twisty sock yarn, so for that end use, I would ply our example singles to 6 twists per inch, which would be about 5 twists per inch when washed—still more twisty

than a balanced yarn but just right for my purposes. The two main ways to measure the amount of twist in a piece of yarn are twists per inch and twist angle.

To find the twists per inch accurately, lay the yarn on a ruler and count how many times a single fiber twists around the yarn in a 1-inch (2.5 cm) length. This is easiest with a larger diameter yarn or a marled yarn (so that the color change makes it easy to see the twist). To find the angle of twist, use a protractor to make a chart. Place the protractor on an index card and draw a baseline. With the protractor set at 0° on that baseline, mark points at 5° increments. Connect these lines to the baseline. To measure the yarn, hold it taut (but not tight enough to distort it). Look at the angle of the fibers as they're twisting and decide which degree line they match best.

This can be hard to see with thin yarns; try using a magnifying glass to see better or lay a needle on the twist line to help pinpoint the twist angle. The angle of twist may change throughout the yarn, but you can get a good estimation. Lower numbers indicate low-twist yarns, while higher degrees are for energized yarns or yarns to be plied. Most of the time, I prefer to decide by feel and eyeballing whether the yarn I'm spinning has the right amount of twist (see page 48).

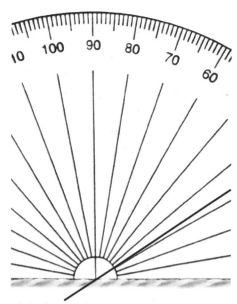

This three-ply yarn has 5½ twists per inch and a twist angle of about 33°.

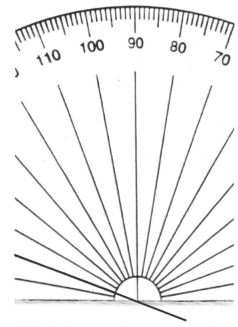

This singles yarn has 10 twists per inch and a twist angle of about 20°.

let's make some yarns!

Learning techniques and practicing skills is all well and good, but the real fun comes from getting down to making yarn. We've discussed the possibilities and variables—types of fiber, drafting and finishing methods, and good spinning habits. This section explores many of my favorite yarns, from singles to cables to funky art yarns, with details on how to make them and how to use them. Try them out, find your own favorites, and use these ideas to make your very own personal dream yarns.

spectacular singles

I have always been in love with good singles—low-twist singles, fulled singles, energized singles. They're fun to make and fun to use. They're essentially not much different from plied yarns, except that you get to use them sooner. They are weaker than plied yarns but used for the right project, they're wonderful. Singles can also be challenging, but armed with the right tools, you'll be able to make consistent singles yarns.

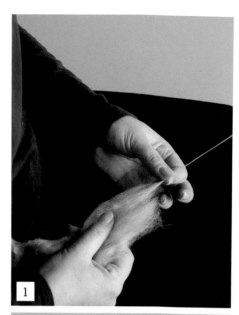

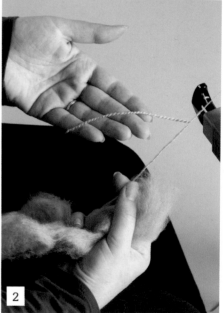

Energized Singles

Energized singles are fun to spin and use. They aren't usually available in commercial yarns, so spinners can make fantastic yarns that money can't buy. Energized singles can be spun in any weight, but I love to make socks or lace with this type of yarn, so I spin it fairly fine. For strength, I use a worsted technique.

To make energized singles, set your wheel for a moderate amount of twist—a ratio between 12:1 for a thicker yarn and 22:1 for a finer yarn. Spin this yarn the same way you would if you were going to use it in a plied yarn—but don't ply it.

Don't set this yarn before using it—use it right off the bobbin. The point is to use a highly energetic yarn, and finishing the yarn will tame some of the twist. If you need to free up your bobbin, don't wind the yarn into a center-pull ball. Pulling the yarn from the center will result in a gnarly mess as the active twist kinks up. (This is a good reason why you don't usually see these yarns available commercially.)

[1] Spin energized singles as if to ply.

[2] The singles should have moderate twist—not too much, not too little.

Bias at Work

The most significant trait of this yarn is that it biases. Spin the singles Z, or left, and it will bias to the right when knitted (as in the green sample); spin it S, or right, and it will bias to the left (as in the peach sample). To counteract the biasing, knit through the back loops (even in ribbing) or work in garter stitch. If you knit with two opposite-twist singles held together, the fabric will lie straight. The bias isn't visible in knitted lace or crochet, though if you have wildly energized singles, you may see some shifting even in lace. A heavy blocking will usually knock out the bias. Energized singles can create interesting and unexpected effects in weaving, so sample before you get started with a big project.

When knitted, energized singles bias in the direction opposite the spinning direction.

Biasing can be overcome in lace knitting (left), crochet (center), or by holding two opposite-twist singles together (right).

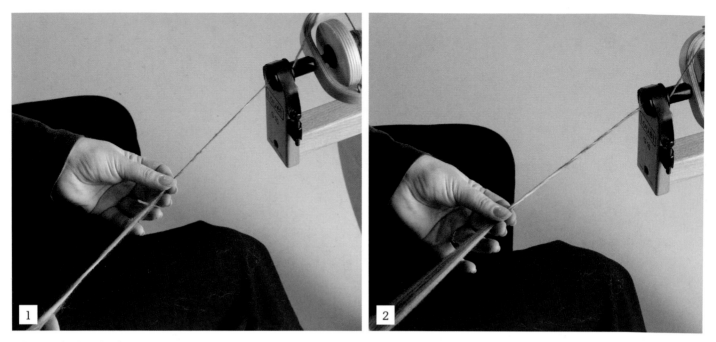

[1] Low-twist singles spun woolen-style. [2] Low-twist singles spun worsted-style.

Low-twist Singles

Low-twist singles are sometimes available commercially, although they are often fulled to make them stronger and ensure that the fibers in the yarn hold together well. (Some commercial yarns that look like singles are actually made up of two singles twisted together in the same direction they were spun in; see page 60 for more on analyzing yarn.)

These yarns can be a challenge for many spinners. How much twist is enough to hold the yarn together without making an unmanageable over-twisted yarn? It's all about finding the right amount of twist per inch (see page 63). For thin low-twist singles, aim for about 2 to 3 twists per inch; for thicker

low-twist singles, you need less than one twist per inch. For thick-and-thin singles, there will be sections of higher and lower twist.

For all low-twist singles, adjust your wheel for a faster uptake and lower twist ratio than you would use to make energized singles or yarns for plying. Don't hold onto the yarn for so long that a lot of twist builds up; let it feed onto the wheel fairly quickly. Choose airy fibers that you can draft easily; you want to be able to choose whether to draft thin or thick. A low-twist singles is one yarn for which it's easy to predraft too much. If you severely strip down the fiber and feed it onto the wheel without drafting, you'll make a heavy, dense yarn.

Also consider the staple of your fibers. Shorter fibers and thinner yarns need more twist than long fibers and fat yarns. This is no less important in a low-twist yarn than a tightly twisted one. Low twist doesn't mean spinning to the same number of twists per inch for every type of fiber. It means that the yarn has low twist relative to that particular fiber type and yarn thickness.

If you are just beginning to experiment with low-twist yarns, practice with longer-staple fibers. It is easier to spin them in a continuous thread, and it will build your confidence and physical memory. When you move on to a more difficult fiber, your hands and feet will have a better idea of how to behave.

Some fibers are not suited for low-twist singles. Although singles made with short-staple fibers can be fulled to hold them together, superwash wool yarns and cotton yarns cannot be fulled. (See page 56 for information on fulling yarn.) These yarns are more likely to fall apart and, in general, shouldn't be used for low-twist singles.

Thin Low-twist Singles

This yarn is wonderful for lace. It's difficult to find from commercial sources, so you have the opportunity to make something unique. The basic process to make it is the same as for other low-twist yarns—use strong draw-in to add less twist. It is especially important to use airy, easily drafted fibers.

Thin low-twist singles yarn is interesting because it's challenging to find the right balance of twist for such a thin yarn. But aside from the spinning challenge in creating a good usable yarn, there's a benefit to the lace knitter: a well-made singles yarn won't split like so many plied lace yarns do.

This yarn can be fulled, but this Romney laceweight singles has enough twist to keep it stable without fulling. If the fibers are long, as in this Romney, and the yarn is well spun, there is no need to full it, though you can if you want assurance it will hold. If you're spinning a shorter-staple fiber and you want to be assured the yarn will hold, then by all means full it.

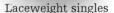

Laceweight singles

Soft Aran-weight singles

Self-striping singles

Low-twist Aran-weight Fulled Woolen Singles

For these soft Aran-weight singles, combining long draw with carded fiber results in a light and lofty singles yarn. It is extremely soft, light, warm, and squishy—definitely a yummy yarn. The woolen draft produces a yarn that is more likely to pill, so fulling it will help prevent some of the pilling and help the fibers in the yarn hold together.

Low-twist Self-striping Fulled Worsted Singles

To spin this yarn, I lined up several colors of wool top in the sequence that I wanted in the finished piece. To make a strong yarn for mittens, hats, or sweaters, I spun the yarn worsted, keeping my feet slow and my hands fast to ensure lower twist. Then I fulled the yarn to make it even stronger. Singles yarns are generally not as strong as plied yarns, but by using a worsted draw and an aggressive fulling wash, you can create fairly durable singles.

Marled Singles

The easiest marled yarn, and the one most often found commercially, is a two-ply made with two different-colored singles. However, you can also make marled singles by holding different colors of fiber side by side and spinning them as low-twist singles. Both sources should be the same kind of fiber prepared in the same way. Don't choose one fiber from top and one from a batt; they will be hard to draft together evenly. Your goal is to draft them at the same rate, keeping the fibers side by side without having sections that are all one color.

Hold two different colors of fiber and draft them together to make marled singles.

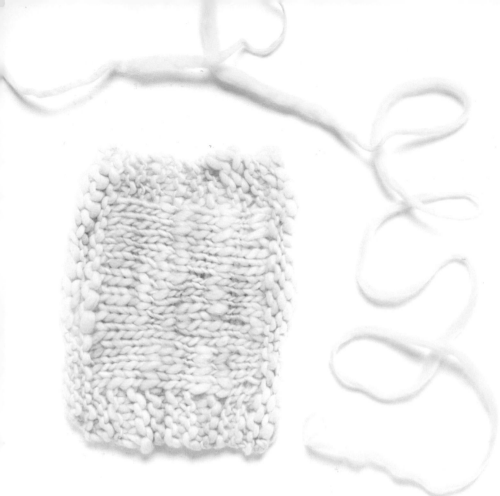

Thick-and-thin Singles

These highly textured yarns could easily fit in the novelty category, but they are basic singles. The first yarn you ever made was likely thick and thin, but many spinners find it hard to go back to their beginner ways when they want to produce this yarn. You can do it with a little practice. There are several ways to make this yarn, depending how comfortable you are with predrafting or drafting on the fly.

To make it without any predrafting, use a fiber that is a bit grabby and resists drafting out smoothly. You will feed the fiber into the orifice fairly fast and keep the twists per inch low so you can create thinner and thicker spots. As you draft, pull the fiber forward unevenly to create clumps, sometimes drawing in front of the drafting triangle, sometimes from behind it. The twist will run toward the thin spots and leave the thicker areas with less twist. This takes a little

bit of abandon if you approach spinning from a technical perspective; it's a real go-with-the-flow yarn. It can be very freeing to make. Thick-and-thin singles can even be made with more than one kind of fiber.

If you find it difficult to spin irregularly on purpose, predraft your fiber just as you want it to spin. If necessary, strip it into narrow pieces and then fluff the strips at intervals. When you begin to spin the fiber, allow the stripped portions onto the wheel without drafting and then draft the fluffed sections to make them thinner. The parts of the fiber that were barely drafted will be a little denser, but it will help you get the feel of making the yarn. With practice, you will eventually be able to make this yarn without manipulating the fiber source.

Finish this yarn with a wash and a snap or two. I don't full this yarn unless the fibers won't stay together otherwise.

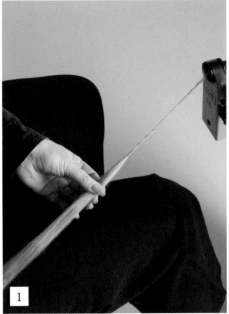

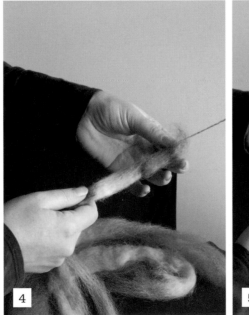

Spinning Thick and Thin

[1–2] Drafting fiber alternately from behind and in front of the drafting triangle creates deliberately thick-and-thin yarn.

[3] To help make thick-and-thin yarn, predraft and prefluff your fiber at intervals.

[4–5] When spinning, draft only the fluffed-out portions, allowing the thicker areas to be spun with little twist.

two-ply: spinners' yarn

Two-ply is the most basic plied yarn, and it's probably the yarn most commonly produced by handspinners. Some spinners may make it almost exclusively. Spinning the plied yarn you want begins in the singles.

Two-ply yarns tend to be flat instead of round. The most common commercial two-ply is lace yarn. The flatness and little nubs along the edges help grab the stitches and hold the lace together. But two-ply is not just for knitters and crocheters; it's also wonderful for weaving.

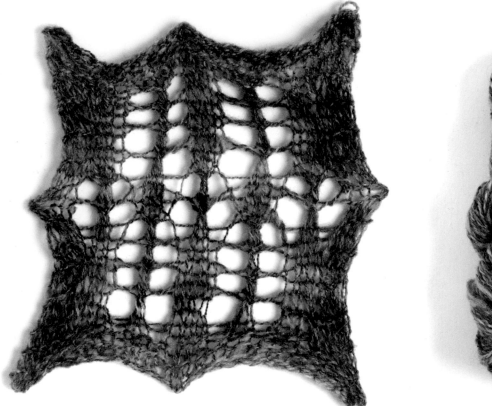

Lace two-ply

Lace Two-ply

You can choose to spin lace yarn worsted-style to make the thin yarn more durable and give the best stitch definition, or you can spin a lovely woolen lace yarn for an airy garment with lots of halo. The most important thing to remember about lace is that thin yarn needs more twist in the singles to hold the fibers together. Using a fiber with a short staple requires even more twist.

Lace yarns are easier to spin with a high ratio. If you don't have a whorl that produces a high ratio or a lace flyer and bobbin, there are a few adjustments

you can make to get enough twist in your singles yarn for a thin two-ply laceweight.

First, use pipe insulation to make a larger core for your bobbin. You may have noticed that you need to increase the tension on your bobbin as it becomes fuller. By making a thicker core for the bobbin, you are using that principle to reduce tension without changing the brake band on your wheel. This modification creates less pull on the yarn, which gives it more time to accumulate enough twist. It also makes the pull-in less strong.

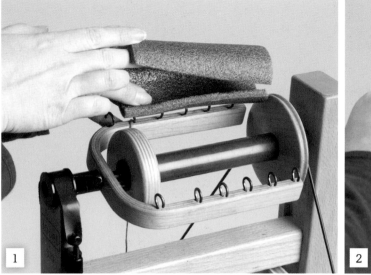

Spinning Fine

[1] Cut a length of foam pipe insulation to fit over the bobbin core.

[2] Lace the yarn through hooks on opposite sides of the flyer.

Second, loop your yarn from one arm of the flyer to the other. This also slows down the draw-in. The more times the yarn crosses the flyer, the slower the draw-in, giving you plenty of time to add more twist.

When plying lace yarn (as with any other yarn), you will need to keep the wheel at the same ratio (or higher) as you used for spinning. Plying lace yarn can seem laborious if you switch to a lower ratio because you won't get enough twist, and you want to be sure to keep the right number of twists per inch. Some yarns that are loosely

plied are fine, but when knitting lace, we often use pointy needles. You don't want to be splitting the plies, or you'll curse your decision to have a loosely plied lace yarn. Many spinners recommend choosing a higher or lower ratio depending on whether you are spinning woolen or worsted yarn, but you will need to decide for yourself. Sampling is the best way for you to decide how your yarn should look and behave. It will also help you see the twist per inch at work in the plying.

The flat, almost barbed, edges of two-ply yarn (far left) make it perfect for lace. The three-ply (near left) is more rounded.

Brushed Two-ply

This yarn is similar to some commercial yarns that are marketed as mohair lace yarn. To make this yarn, spin mohair singles and nylon singles as you would any fibers that are going to be plied. The mohair in the sample yarn at right was spun woolen-style for maximum halo effect. Brushing a woolen yarn will produce more poof in less brushing time. The nylon was spun worsted-style for strength, with the wheel adjusted for a high-twist ratio with a moderate draw-in. This yarn can be as thin or thick as you want it. (If you'd rather not spin nylon, choose a commercial nylon thread.)

The trick to making this yarn comes when you get to the finishing steps. Ply the singles together normally and then set the twist. When the yarn is dry, use a natural-bristle brush to stroke lightly along the length of the yarn. This will create the classic fluffy halo of mohair yarns. If you are nervous about damaging your yarn by brushing, you can brush the fabric after knitting instead (or in addition) to create more halo.

Mohair isn't the only fiber that can be brushed to create a halo; alpaca also makes a great brushed yarn. The sample below is made from one ply of worsted-spun Corriedale and one ply of woolen-spun alpaca.

Brushed alpaca and Corriedale

Brushed mohair and nylon

Creating a Brushed Yarn

[1] After spinning, the yarn is fairly smooth.

[2] Use a natural-bristle brush to stroke the yarn.

[3] After brushing, the yarn is fuzzy and has a warm halo.

80% Merino/20% angora

Angora Two-ply

As little as 20% angora can be plenty to enhance the luxury, warmth, and look of a yarn (see page 19). These two yarns show the difference between blended angora and 100% angora—but don't take my word for it. Experiment with different amounts of angora or other short, fluffy fiber. The pink sample was spun worsted from a combed top that was 80% Merino/20% angora. The blue sample is 100% angora.

100% angora

Self-striping two-ply with gradual transitions

Set Up to Self-Stripe
Divide the top so that each piece has the same color pattern.

Self-striping Two-ply

This technique takes a bit of finagling, but there are a few simple tricks that will help make a self-striping two-ply yarn from a handpainted top or roving. First, recognize the pattern in your fiber. Most handpainted fiber is dyed with a regular pattern or repeat. Break the fiber into pieces that have the same pattern and lay them out. (You could also split

handpainted fiber lengthwise, keeping the two halves as even as possible, though it is often difficult to divide evenly this way.) Above I have four roughly equal pieces; for a two-ply yarn, that gives me two sections per bobbin. Spin the bobbins as evenly as you can, matching the diameter of the singles on each bobbin and keeping track of the order of the color sequence.

How you ply will depend on how important it is that the singles change color at exactly the same place. If you want a gradual shift from one color to another (as in the sample above), simply ply the yarns together; for the most part the colors should transition evenly. If you really don't want any color overlapping, you'll probably need to break one of the singles and splice to match up the colors (see page 51).

Corriedale/tussah with
silk noil, spun woolen

Silky Tweed

Tweed is all about the fiber, and the yarn
can be spun in many ways. The fiber is
usually a solid or semisolid color with
bits of fiber in other colors in it. Fiber
for tweeds is mostly available as roving
and batts. You won't usually see this as
a combed top because the combing
process is meant to take out the little
bits and neps that give tweeds their
texture and look.

The kind of tweedy look you want
will determine how you choose fiber
for a particular project. Tweed blends
can come with tiny neps all the way
up to large blob-like neps. The typical
tweed on the commercial market has
moderate to small neps. Be aware of
what you're getting and you will be
happy with the finished product.

Tweed is not as well suited for a singles
yarn that is not fulled. The little neps are
likely to fall out faster without fulling.

Bluefaced Leicester with
silk noil, spun worsted

Although tweed singles may have lots of lumps and bumps, plying will tend to even them out. By the time you have a three- or four-ply yarn, it may be relatively even and smooth.

To create the soft, lovely purple tweed above left, I began by carding purple Corriedale with tussah silk. I added silk noils on the first pass through the drumcarder so that they would be well integrated. Incorporating the noil thoroughly in the batt doesn't always mean it will stay secure in the final yarn, but it does help. It also helps to disperse the tweed into flecks instead of giant clumps, which will fall out faster. I spun the purple yarn from rolag-style chunks into a true woolen yarn (see pages 32–33 and 44). Although tweed can be spun worsted or woolen, I wanted the softness of this blend to be enhanced by the spinning method.

The sage sample is made of Bluefaced Leicester with silk noils. I used a worsted draw to keep the noils in place as much as possible. Since the fibers are carded, the yarn can be considered semiwoolen; it cannot be a true worsted-style yarn.

Plying from Both Ends

If you're making a two-ply yarn and have a bunch of singles left on one bobbin, you can wind a center-pull ball or make an Andean plying bracelet. (An Andean plying bracelet isn't comfortable for a large quantity of yarn.) Splice both ends of the yarn on your wrist or center-pull ball to the yarn on the bobbin and finish up that last bit.

[1] To start an Andean plying bracelet, anchor one end of the yarn and wrap it in front of your thumb and index finger and around your middle finger.

[2] Bring the yarn toward your thumb to the back of your hand, then across the back.

[3] From the palm of your hand below your pinkie, wrap the yarn around your middle finger, back toward the pinkie, and across the back again.

[4] Bring the yarn forward, around the middle finger, and to the back again. Repeat until all the yarn is used up. For your comfort, wrap loosely.

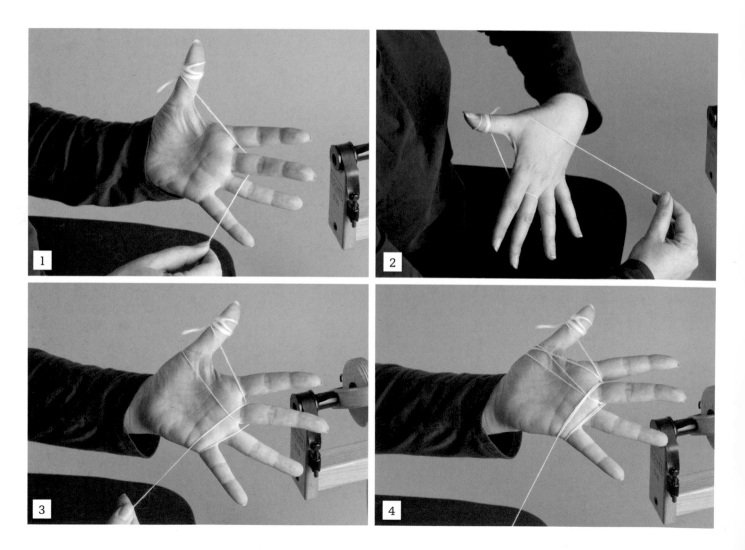

[5] When looking at the back of your hand, you should see yarn only straight across below the thumb and pinkie and around the middle finger.

[6] When looking at your palm, you should see yarn only in diagonal lines from your thumb and pinkie toward your middle finger—none crosses the palm directly.

[7] Gently remove your middle finger from the yarn, leaving the rest of the bracelet in place and disturbing it as little as possible.

[8] Attach both ends of the yarn to the bobbin and use your wrapped hand to manage the singles while the other hand drafts for plying as usual.

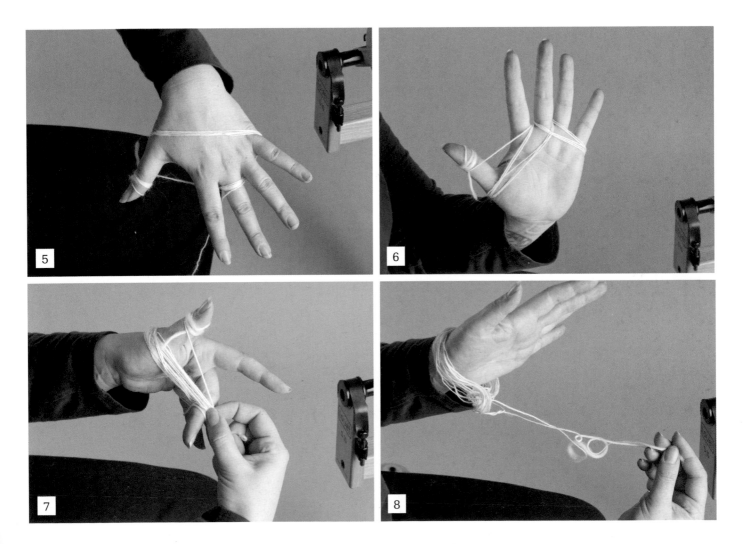

three (or more) plies

Making three-ply, four-ply, or more-ply yarn isn't much different in principle from making two-ply yarn. And you don't have to stop with four plies—experiment and have fun. Dream big! The biggest consideration when plying more than two strands of yarn is that it can be difficult to keep even tension on all the strands. Some spinners find it helpful to use an aid (sometimes called a plying template) to keep the strands separated, such as the inner lid of a spice jar or a button with large holes. Pass each of the singles through a separate hole in the tool and hold it forward, keeping the twist from entering the plies unevenly.

Multiple Plies

If it's more difficult to ply more than two strands, why do it? For one thing, three-ply and four-ply yarns are rounder, which is fantastic for stitch definition. They look incredible knitted in cable patterns; cables "pop" when knitted in multi-ply yarns. For the same reason, multi-ply yarns are also great for color work (see page 22). Multi-ply yarns are perfect for spinners who like to make incredibly thin singles. It's a great way to make strong and professional-looking yarn while making it thicker and stronger. The more plies, the more regular the yarn becomes.

Let's revisit the technical examples from page 63 to understand the effect of adding more plies on the twists per inch. To ply three singles that are each 12 twists per inch, a balanced plied yarn should have 4 twists per inch. For a four-ply with the same singles, we'd aim for 3 twists per inch, technically speaking. In my everyday spinning, I use the plyback test first to tell whether I have the right amount of twist. As for two-ply yarn, I often prefer slightly overplied yarns. Once you sample a few yarns, you will develop your own preferences.

Woolen Three-ply

Woolen yarns tend to be warm and lofty. They make fantastic outerwear, although they don't hold up as well as worsteds, so it's best to consider wear and tear and where you need the warmth more than the strength. To make warm yarn (the green sample above right) to be knitted into mittens, I blended wool from a local fleece pool with a bit of sparkle. For maximum warmth, I used a long draw for a true woolen yarn.

Worsted Four-ply

More plies make a stronger yarn—both in tensile strength (resistance to breaking) and abrasion (resistance to pilling). This is especially true for worsted yarns. For the four-ply yarn below right, I made singles in each of four different colors of top. (Flexibility is one of the best things about making your own yarn—you are in charge of the color.) This worsted yarn is smooth, crisp, and strong, with each of the colors well defined.

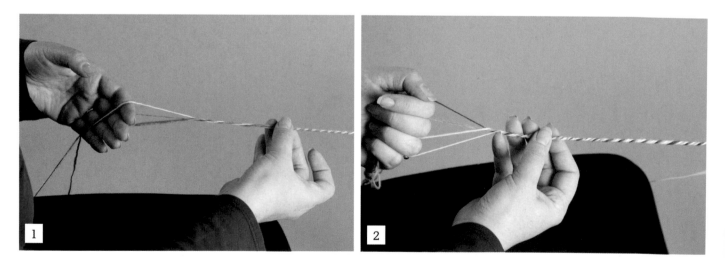

Plying Three (or More) Strands

[1] Use your fingers or another tool to keep the strands separated and under equal tension before the twist enters.

[2] To ply more strands, just continue to hold them apart with your back hand.

Woolen three-ply

*If you're short on bobbins,
wind off your yarn onto storage
bobbins, into center-pull balls,
or onto cardboard cores. This is
a good idea if you don't fill your
bobbins evenly when spinning.

Worsted three-ply

Navajo or Chain Plying

Although this method is commonly called Navajo plying, it is easier to envision if you think "chain ply." You are essentially making a crochet chain from one bobbin of singles while adding ply twist. There is much contention in the spinning community about what to call this particular yarn, but it is an interesting technique no matter what you call it.

Chain plying has advantages and disadvantages, just like any other yarn. On the plus side, it requires only one bobbin of singles and is worked until that bobbin is empty (or you want to stop)—there are no leftovers, and fancy measuring is not required to make plying from bobbins come out even. It also preserves the color order of your singles. Like other multi-ply yarns, Navajo-plied yarns are less likely to pill. The main disadvantage is that the yarn is weaker than a true three-ply yarn. The little joins where a new loop of the chain begins are the weakest points. Additionally, it's structurally only one piece of yarn, so if one strand breaks, the whole yarn can ravel. If one ply breaks on a true three-ply, there are still two strands there, and it's much easier to fix.

To start, spin a singles yarn. If you spin a highly overtwisted yarn, you'll likely be cursing as the yarn winds up on itself, but if it doesn't have enough twist, you will be cursing as the yarn falls apart during plying. You want medium twist; you may find it easiest to make over-twisted yarn and let it sit for a few days to settle.

After spinning the singles and setting up the bobbin in the lazy kate, attach the yarn to the leader with a large knotted loop. Hold the knot with your forward hand. With your back hand, reach from the top down through the loop, pick up the singles strand, and pull it through forming a new loop. Start the wheel in the plying direction (S). Use the forward hand to hold the original loop and the singles apart under tension, keeping the twist in check.

Your back hand is still holding the new loop of the singles that you pulled through the first loop. When the twist is partway up the three strands, use your back hand to reach through the new loop and pull up another loop of singles.

You may recognize this as a crochet chain. There will be little nubs where one loop ends and another is pulled through. At the beginning the nubs may be large, but as you practice making this yarn they will get smaller. When you use the yarn, the nubs are not noticeable.

Chain Plying

[1] To begin chain plying, tie a large knotted loop and hold it open.

[2] Reach through the loop, pick up the singles, and draw it through, forming another loop. (The knot is visible at the front of the loop.)

[3] Turn the wheel in the plying direction and allow the twist to enter all three strands.

Repeat Steps 2–3 until all the yarn is plied.

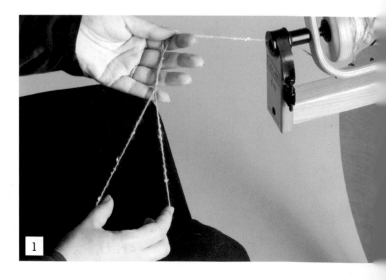

When you are first chain plying, you may find that you make short, small loops, and as you continue your loops get bigger. If the loops are oversize, they may tangle easily. It takes practice, but I find it fun to do, even when I'm not after a particular color effect.

Chain-plied Self-striping Yarn

The most common reason to chain-ply is to keep the stripes in your singles intact. The sample yarn above was made from one piece of handpainted superwash Corriedale that was spun with long color repeats and chain-plied to create stripes. Put enough twist in the singles to make a durable sock yarn after chain plying. When plying, make the loops large or small as needed to preserve the color sections and make sure none of the colors overlap.

Chain-plied self-striping Corriedale

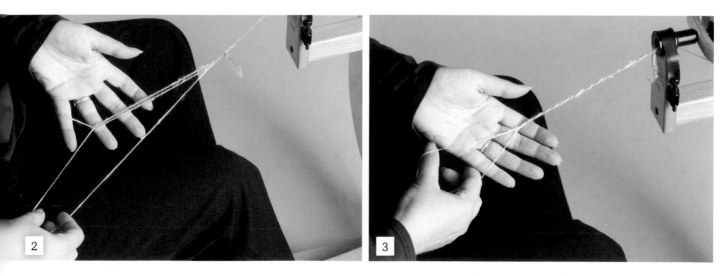

Cables

Cables are made by plying two or more singles together, then plying two or more of those together in the opposite direction to make one yarn. The most basic of these is a four-stranded cable made from two two-plies. Note that when you cable ply, you don't add twist again in the plying direction; each time you combine yarns, you add twist in the opposite direction. In other words, if you originally spun the yarn clockwise (Z) and plied it counterclockwise (S), you would cable clockwise (Z).

If you are going to cable a yarn, make sure the yarns that you are using have been overplied, but keep in mind the rules of twists per inch and plying (see page 63). For example, if you have a singles with 16 twists per inch, a balanced ply will have 8 twists per inch, but you want it to be overplied, so choose to ply at 10 to 12 twists per inch. Then, when you cable, use the rules of balanced yarn to ply at 5 to 6 twists per inch.

If you aren't excited about plying, cabling might seem like the bane of your existence. Why would you keep plying? Cabled yarn has incredible definition. If you think three- and four-ply yarns have great stitch definition, you need to see cabled yarns in action. Knitted cables seem to just pop out and say hello when worked in cabled yarn.

As with any yarn, there are a few drawbacks. It takes a lot of time to make a cabled yarn (which you might consider a positive or a negative). Depending on the project you're planning, you may not want that crisp, well-defined stitch. As with all spinning, it's all about making the right yarn for the job.

The three samples above right demonstrate some of the unique properties of cables. The red-and-white yarn at near right is a cable composed of the two two-ply yarns to its right. The cable is

Four-strand cable
and components

smoother and more consistent than the fluffy two-ply yarns. However, despite the fact that it contains twice as much fiber as its two-ply components, it actually has a smaller diameter than either. (Not every cabled yarn will be thinner than the yarns it was made from, but these two woolen-spun yarns were substantially compacted by cabling.)

Making a four-strand cable is as simple as twisting two two-ply yarns in the direction opposite the way they were plied.

Four-strand
worsted cable

Nine-strand cable

Four-strand Cable

This is the simplest cabled yarn. It is made with two worsted-spun two-ply yarns that are cabled together. The sample shows how well the pattern stands out with this type of yarn. Can you imagine how good this yarn would make your next colorwork or cabled project look? Four-strand cable is extremely durable and will really make that project pop.

Nine-strand Navajo-plied Cable

This yarn started as an experiment. I spun three solid colors from batts into singles, then Navajo-plied each of them. I put the three bobbins on the kate and cabled them together (in the same direction that they were spun as singles). The resulting yarn is very round and strong.

You don't need to stop with nine plies—you can keep going with this. There is one commercial yarn that is a six-stranded cable made from three two-ply yarns. I even found a twenty-strand cable made from five four-ply yarns. Experiment and have fun—cable plying is incredibly interesting.

core spinning and more

until now, all the yarns I have mentioned have been made from one or more singles, spun in the same direction; plying has been with similar singles, even tension, and in the direction opposite that of the singles. While these are the bread-and-butter techniques that many spinners use exclusively, great things can happen when you mix in other elements, such as unspun fibers and plies held under different tension. There are infinite variations and choices of materials, but the reasons for making a corespun yarn will help you decide what materials to use.

Core Spinning

Core spinning produces a wide range of yarns with two common elements: a strong core and an outer layer of unspun fiber.

Choose a durable core. Depending on what kind of yarn you're making, it needs to have the right amount of twist, be twisted in the right direction, and be strong enough to hold up to both you and the wheel tugging on it at the same time.

A core can be anything from crochet cotton to nylon thread to an ugly yarn that you want to cover up. The amount of twist needed in the core depends on whether you are planning to twist it in the same direction it was spun (for which you want a low-twist yarn to avoid kinking) or the opposite direction (for which you need high twist to keep the core from coming apart). When you decide on a core, you may need to remove or add twist before you can use it.

The outer layer may be any fiber you can get your hands on. The fiber that you choose and the yarn you want will dictate how much twist you need and how you will add it to the core.

Core spinning is especially useful if you have a delicate fiber that you want to strengthen. The core makes these yarns much stronger than other yarns. For example, using angora for warp thread can be risky, but core-spun angora will resist breakage while still providing a luxurious texture.

Tease out a bit of fiber that you are going to use around your core. Attach the core thread or yarn and your fiber to your leader. Hold the core firmly with your back hand and hold the outer layer with your front hand at a 60° to 90° angle to the core so that it will wrap around the core completely.

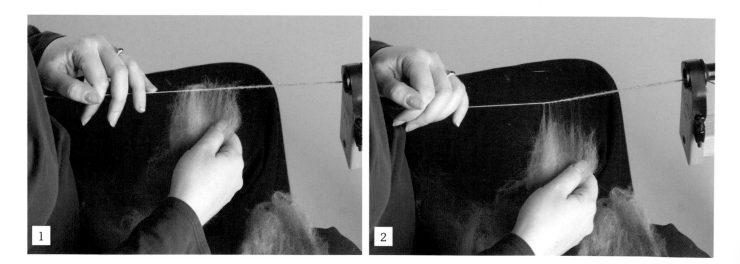

Core Spinning

[1] Hold the fiber against the core at a 60° to 90° angle.

[2] As twist is added to the core, it will trap the fiber in a fluffy outer layer.

Start the wheel spinning in the correct direction. Correct direction depends on the type of yarn you want to end up with and the core you are using. Generally, you want to twist in the same direction in which the core was spun. If you are using a core of crochet cotton that was plied Z, then spin Z. As twist is added to the core, the outer layer is trapped with it. I keep a firm hold on the core with my back hand and continue to keep the fiber in the front fluffy so it will attach to the core.

Holding the core firmly doesn't mean resisting the wheel, but the core needs to be held more tightly than the outer layer. As discussed in the section on plying (see page 49), yarns must be held under equal tension to be plied evenly. When core spinning, however, the outer layer should be held loosely so that it will wrap around the core.

Basic Core-spun Yarn

For this yarn, I chose a pink crochet cotton core and a Merino top for the outer layer. Because the top was a little condensed, I split it in half lengthwise and swung it in the air to fluff it up and make it easy to draft. I spun the two together in the same direction that the crochet cotton was last twisted.

Corespun Merino

Core-spun Locks

Core spinning can also be used to produce a novelty lock yarn. Holding a bunch of locks in your lap or in a basket within easy reach, begin twisting the core and add the locks as the outer layer. You can pinch and pull the ends of the locks away from the core to keep them from lying flat. This yarn is soft and fluffy, but the core makes it a tough and usable yarn.

To make this fabulous yarn even funkier, ply two bobbins of it together in the direction opposite the core spinning. Plying will help lock in any flyaway fibers and make the yarn resistant to shedding.

Core-spun mohair locks

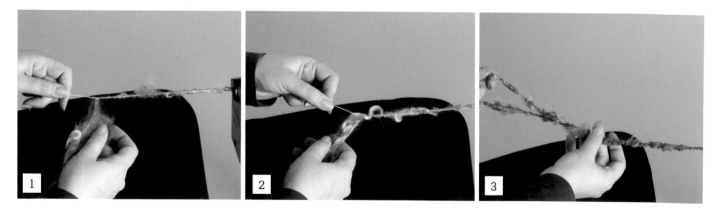

[1] Hold a few locks against the core, trapping them in place.

[2] Pull the ends of the locks away from the core to help them stand out.

[3] Plying two strands of this yarn together will make it less likely to shed.

Elastic-core Spinning

Yet another fabulous way to make core-spun yarn is to use an elastic core. Attach the elastic to the leader as you would any other core and hold it taut but not stretched to capacity while you add the outer layer. The yarn may look odd and springy, but it makes fantastic cuffs for items like mittens, slippers, or socks.

The pink sample is made of Bluefaced Leicester top, and the blue sample uses an angora blend.

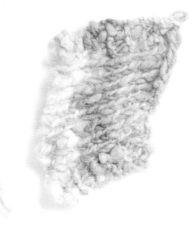

Angora/wool blend, corespun with elastic core

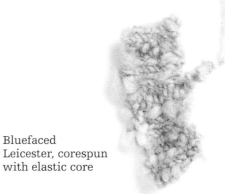

Bluefaced Leicester, corespun with elastic core

[1] Attach the elastic to the leader and hold it taut.

[2] Hold the fiber against the elastic and allow it to be trapped.

[3] When the yarn is relaxed, it is appealingly springy.

Core Plying

Core plying involves using essentially the same techniques as core spinning, with one difference: yarn instead of fiber wraps around the core. Spin one bobbin of singles as you would for a two-ply yarn. The coiled yarn can be delicate or chunky, depending on the diameter of the singles.

Adjust the wheel for moderate draw-in and low twist. As for regular plying, add twist in the opposite direction that you spun the singles in. Hold the singles at a 60° to 90° angle to the core (crochet cotton in this sample). Hold the singles fairly loosely and allow it to loop around the core. Don't let it create loose loops; the coiling yarn should be fairly snug on the core. If necessary, push the coils up to wrap them closer together.

Coils and Bobbles

For a coiled yarn (above right), spin a bobbin of singles with the same amount of twist you would use for plying. For the coils to be even, the singles should be even.

For a bobble yarn (right), spin thick-and-thin singles for the wrapping yarn and push the thick sections so they snug together on the core. Hold the core fairly taut.

This yarn is really interesting when worked up; it is a yarn that I use for decoration (and the pleasure of making it) as well as for knitting. There's no better centerpiece than a lovely bowl full of yarn skeins and balls.

Coil yarn

Bobble yarn

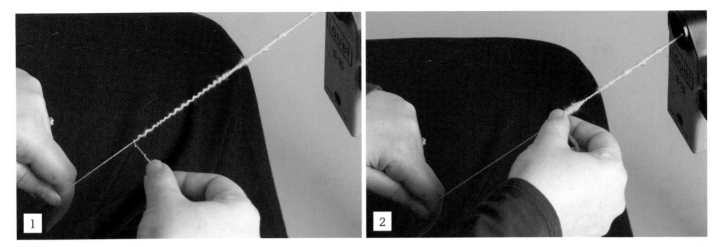

Making Coils

[1] For coiled yarn, core-ply a bobbin of even singles. Hold the singles loosely at a 60° to 90° angle to the core and let it wrap around.

[2] If necessary, push the loops up on the core.

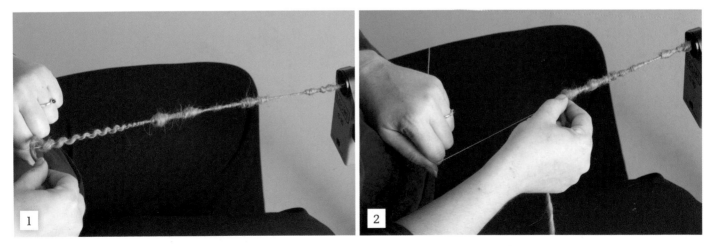

Making Bobbles

[1] For bobble yarn, core-ply a bobbin of thick-and-thin singles.

[2] Push the coils up on the yarn to create bobbles.

Bouclé

Bouclé consists of three elements: the core, the loopy layer, and the top binder. These can be put together in a variety of combinations, though the loopy layer is best in a fiber such as mohair or a longwool such as Wensleydale or Lincoln. These glossy long-staple fibers make crisp, shiny loops.

To start, spin three sets of singles, one spun S (counterclockwise) with low twist, one spun S (counterclockwise) with high twist, and one spun Z (clockwise) with high twist. First, attach two yarns to the leader, the low-twist S-spun singles and the Z-spun singles, and begin spinning counterclockwise (S). Hold the low-twist yarn taut and the Z-twist yarn at a 60° to 90° angle, allowing the Z-twist yarn to wrap loosely around the core. Unlike coil yarn, where the loops were pushed snug against each other and the core, the wraps for bouclé should be loose and messy. You can push the loops forward on the core to add more loops, although they should not completely cover the core; the more loops added now, the curlier and funkier the final yarn.

This yarn tends to get caught in the flyer hooks and sometimes the orifice of the wheel. If that happens, just guide it past the snag; you will have a chance in the next step to correct this.

Next, set up this messy-looking yarn to ply with the remaining high-twist S singles, which is the binder. Start the wheel spinning Z (clockwise) and hold both the curl-covered yarn and the binder singles under equal tension. The binder is added as a "normal" ply, without one yarn held out at an angle. Although the tension is even, you may need to use one hand to arrange the loops in a pleasing manner. This can be tricky; I hold both yarns in one hand and use the other hand to rearrange the loops and keep it all even. The loops can be moved around easily

before plying with the binder, but once the binder yarn is added, the loops are securely in place.

It can be interesting to make a yarn that is a partial bouclé, alternating loopy and nonloopy areas. Play with colors and textures and make samples. Bouclés offer a lot of opportunities to experiment. They are time-consuming, especially if they get caught in the spinning wheel frequently, but they're also rewarding. Small amounts of bouclé can be used as accents to dress up an otherwise plain piece.

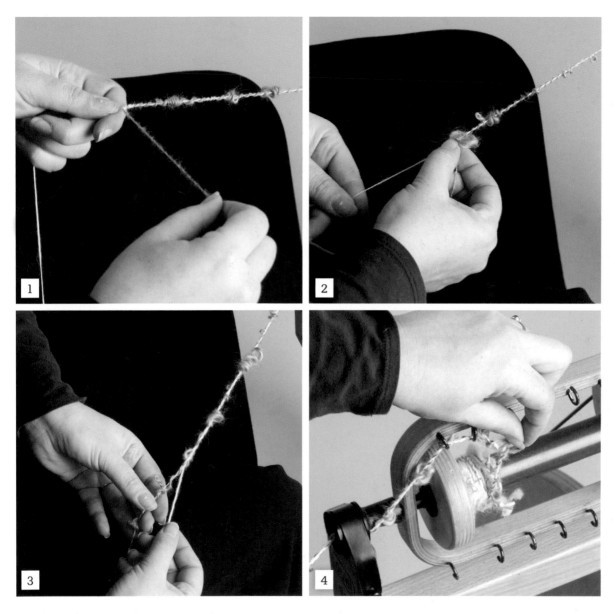

Spinning Bouclé

[1] With the wheel turning counterclockwise (S), hold the low-twist yarn taut, with the Z-spun singles held loosely to the side at a 60° to 90° angle.

[2] If desired, push the loops forward on the core so that you can add more loops.

[3] Twist the looped yarn with the remaining singles clockwise (Z).

[4] Be careful not to catch the loops on the hooks of the flyer; move the yarn by hand if necessary.

novelty yarns

A whole world of variety opens up when you change the fiber content and the spinning techniques of your yarns. All of the yarns described here are easy to use in projects and are fun to make without getting too wild. These are yarns that you almost certainly won't find on the commercial market. Use the following ideas to build your skills and then begin experimenting with wild ideas of your own.

Plying Effects

Eclectic plying uses the techniques for typical plying but applies them to something a little more unusual. Plying very different kinds of singles or singles with another element can create different and surprisingly effective results. It might sound like just an exercise in matching up unlike items by running them through the wheel, but much of making effectively unique plied yarn comes with practice.

Ewelash

This is a handspun-only variation on commercial eyelash yarns. As a beginning plyer, you may have made bits of yarn simliar to this by accident—you might not have known it could be a desireable novelty yarn if you let go of the notion of plying "perfectly"!

Start by spinning two bobbins of singles in the Z direction, one with a typical twist amount (as for plying) and the other overtwisted and with about one-third more yardage than the other. Attach both singles to the leader and start to ply in the S direction. Hold one singles in each hand, keeping the two under equal tension. After a few inches (or the desired length), relax the tension on the overtwisted singles so you can see it twist up on itself and then resume even tension and "capture" the tail by plying normally. Continue to alternate

Ewelash yarn

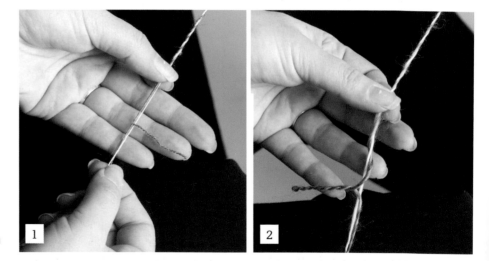

Spinning Ewelash

[1] Relax the overtwisted singles, allowing a small pigtail to twist back on itself.
[2] Resume plying the two singles with equal tension.

the tension in the overtwisted singles at even or irregular intervals. The more you do this, the funkier your yarn will be.

Plying with Thread or Yarn

Spin a thick or thick-and-thin woolen singles with medium twist. It is best to use wool for this yarn, because you want something fluffy that will hold its shape. Silk and mohair are too dense and won't give the same effect. Find a contrasting or complementary commercial thread and determine which direction it was spun in. Some commercial threads are just attenuated, not twisted; some are S-spun and some are Z-spun. Match the direction in which you spin your singles to the direction that the commercial thread was last spun in. (If the yarn is attenuated, it can be spun in either direction.)

The thread is super thin and slippery, while the wool is puffy and thick, as at left. Set up the handspun and the thread for plying and then keep the tension even and make a standard two-ply. Many spinners will find it challenging to keep even tension on two very different yarns and may tend to make a core-plied yarn instead of a true two-ply. You could use a thin worsted singles instead of the thread, as at right, which would be slightly easier because the wool will not be as slippery as thread.

Handspun and thread

Thick-and-thin woolen with thin worsted

Commercial to Handspun

You can also create great effects by pairing an interesting commercial yarn like bouclé or eyelash with your handspun. If you have a plethora of yarn left from the eyelash craze, try it—it makes a very interesting yarn when plied with a handspun singles (far right). The only trick to this is to determine the direction in which the commercial yarn was spun. Some commercial yarns are attenuated (meaning they have no Z or S spin), some are S-spun, and some are Z-spun. Keep in mind that the direction the commercial yarn was spun in should be the same direction in which you spin your singles. Spin your singles with a medium amount of twist and then ply it with the commercial yarn. Voilà— easy, funky, one-of-a-kind yarn.

Plying Handspun and Commercial Thread

Attach your singles and the thread to the bobbin and turn the wheel in the plying direction. Hold the commercial thread and the fluffy singles under even tension while plying.

Sequined two-ply

Beaded two-ply

Add-ins

Making yarn with add-ins can be some of the most fun that is legal for spinners. What can you think of that you'd like to add to your yarn? Let your imagination run wild but consider a few physical limitations. There have been a few times when I've gotten all set up to add something fun and weird to my yarn, only to realize that it won't go through the orifice. When that happens, I change wheels or break out the spindle I keep on hand for just this type of job.

Strung Add-ins

Anything you can string on a bobbin of handspun singles or a commercial thread can become part of your yarn! As long as it can stay on the thread and fit through your wheel's orifice, any beads, spangles, and flowers you can dream up can become part of a beautiful custom-made handspun.

BEADS AND SEQUINS

Beaded or sequined yarns can easily dress up a project by adding a hint of sparkle. Unlike beads that are applied while knitting, these yarns are all ready to go when you begin knitting—no need for a tiny crochet hook or a bead spinner when you sit down to knit. A few yarn companies make this type of yarn commercially, but you can combine yarn and beads or sequins to suit your own taste. This technique works with seed beads, textured beads, all kinds of sequins or paillettes, and even charms.

To make beaded or sequined yarn with handspun, spin two sets of singles as for any regular two-ply yarn—but make sure at least one of the yarns is thin enough to fit through the holes of the beads or sequins. The yarn that will hold the beads should also be strong and fairly smooth. A smooth worsted singles is best for reducing risk of breakage and for minimizing wear on the yarn caused by moving beads. The beads shouldn't fit too tightly either, or pulling the yarn through the hole may cause it to break.

String the beads or sequins onto one or both sets of singles. You may need to thread one end of the singles on a needle to pass it through the holes easily. Be sure to string enough beads or sequins for embellishing the full length of the yarn.

Set up the singles for plying. Your back hand will hold most of the beads or sequins back, pushing them forward one at a time at whatever interval you like.

Instead of two handspun singles, this can also be done with one bobbin of handspun and one strand of commercial thread. Thread can be easier to use with beads or sequins because it is thin, strong, and consistent. Spin your singles in the same direction that the thread was last spun in, string the beads onto the thread, and ply them as for two bobbins of handspun.

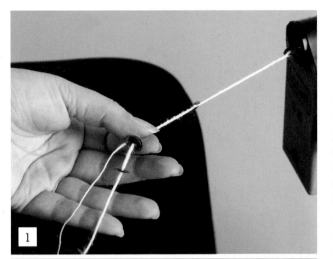

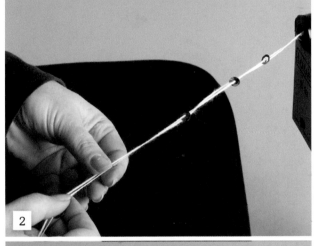

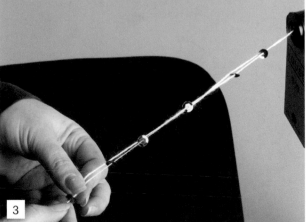

Adding Beads and Sequins

[1] String beads or sequins onto one or both of the singles and attach them to the bobbin.

[2] Ply the singles, using your left hand to keep the beads or sequins back.

[3] Push the beads or sequins forward one by one at regular intervals.

FELTED BEADS, FLOWERS, AND POM-POMS

Beads and sequins are easy add-ins because they have holes that make them easy to string, but you can securely add felted beads, silk flowers, or other items that can be pierced with a needle into your yarn. Spin your singles and then choose a complementary-colored thread and flowers or soft items. Thread a needle and string your add-ins, piercing them either in the center or at a spot that will hold them securely and position them to look their best. For silk flowers, I prefer to tear apart the petals and pass through the centers or through the intact base of the flower. Set up the yarn and thread for plying as for the beaded yarn.

Two-ply with pom-poms

Flowered yarn

Adding Flowers and Pom-poms

[1] Use a needle to string the add-ons onto a complementary thread.

[2] Your back hand will manage the add-ins, pushing them forward to be plied at intervals.

[3] The flowers or beads may get caught going through the orifice; gently pull them through.

Loose Add-ins

Even if the treasure you want to add to your yarn can't be strung on yarn or thread, you can add it with the magic of twist. By inserting items in the yarn while plying, you can take advantage of the forces that hold the plies together to keep feathers, fabric, and bits of yarn in place.

Two-ply with
yarn add-ins

LOCKS, SCRAPS, AND FABRIC

These yarns rely on the power of twist to make the add-ins part of the yarn instead of using a thread passing through them. Prepare a small pile of items to add in—locks, snippets of other yarns, small pieces of fabric—before you sit down to ply so that you won't run out before you are done with your yarn. Spin your singles as for a regular two-ply yarn, set up to ply, and begin to ply for a foot or so. With one hand, maintain tension on both strands of yarn and hold them apart; the other hand will hold a piece of the add-in at the tip of the drafting triangle. Allow the twist to run through the yarns, locking the add-in in place. Continue at regular or irregular intervals as you like. Locks and pieces of yarn will likely stay in place between the plies, but items like cloth might not stay as well. If you're concerned about them being secure, add another layer of twist, either by cabling two lengths of the add-in yarn (see page 94) or by adding a binder as for a bouclé (see page 104).

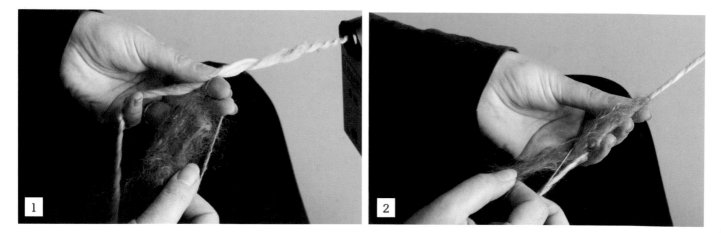

Adding Locks

[1] Hold the yarns apart while placing the add-in between the strands.

[2] Allow the twist to run through the singles and add-in, locking it in place.

FEATHERS

I've saved one of my favorite yarns for last. The method I use to add feathers is a cross between regular plying and core plying. It's not limited to feathers alone; use it to add locks, cloth, or anything else you can dream up.

Spin a high-twist singles yarn in the same direction as a complementary binder thread or yarn. Prepare a pile of feathers to add in. I prefer feathers that are 2 to 4 inches (5–10 cm) in length with a small quill that isn't too hard. The plying technique helps keep the feather's quill from popping out and poking you, but it is best to find feathers with soft quills.

Attach the singles and binder to the leader as for a regular two-ply and ply for about a foot. Holding the singles taut, lay a feather flat against the yarn with the quill end away from you. Hold the binder loosely and let it wrap the yarn and feather together as if core plying. To hold the feather in place, start to wrap in front of the quill, catching some of the downy parts of the feathers. Resume plying normally until you want to add another feather.

I prefer to wrap only part of the feather, leaving most of it free, but you can wrap the whole feather if you like. After all, this is *your* designer yarn! Just make sure to wrap the quill well so it doesn't poke out and stab you.

Feathered yarn

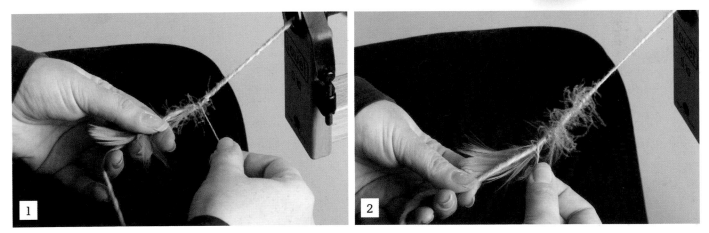

Adding Feathers

[1] With a feather laid against the handspun singles, allow the binder to wrap around the quill.

[2] Wrap some of the down of the feather to catch it securely.

glossary

Batt
A fiber preparation produced on a drumcarder that resembles a blanket; more aligned than a rolag.

Blocking
Similar to blocking a garment or fabric, stretching or using weight to fix fibers in shape. If you are making a weaving yarn, you may want to block your yarn to remove all stretch and have it hang without any energy.

Cable
Four- (or more) strand yarn that is created by two or more two- (or more) ply yarns twisted together in the direction opposite the way they were last twisted.

Cloud prep
A fiber preparation that looks like clouds. It's fluffy and unlike any of the other preps.

Commercial yarn
Yarn that is milled on machines; also called millspun.

Control card
An informational card with a sample of yarn that will help you to make the same yarn in the same grist over and over.

Crimp
The texture or waves that you see in a lock of wool. It varies between breeds.

Double draft
A method of drafting that is akin to long draw for the first draft and short draw for the second.

Double drive
A type of wheel that uses one long drive band that goes to the bobbin and the flyer whorl.

Drafting
The process of pulling out fibers to be twisted into yarn when you are spinning at the wheel or spindle.

Drafting triangle
The triangle-shaped area where twist (yarn) meets the fiber supply.

Energized
Yarn that has excess twist/energy.

Gilled sliver
Similar to pin-drafted roving, a carded fiber that has been processed further to be well aligned.

Irish tension
A single-drive wheel where the bobbin is driven and the flyer is braked.

Marled
Generally two single yarns of different colors twisted together; can also be a singles made from two different colored fibers twisted much the same as two yarns are or can be a cabled yarn.

Novelty yarn
Generally, any yarn that has interesting texture or features that distinguish it from "regular" singles or plied yarns.

Pencil roving
Roving that has been produced in a much smaller strand than traditional roving. The strands are usually the thickness of a marker or pencil.

Pin-drafted roving
Carded fiber that has been drafted through a series of pins, producing a lofty and somewhat aligned preparation, often with a slight twist.

Plying template
A piece of wood, plastic, or metal that has holes in it. It helps you keep singles separated to aid in plying.

Predrafting

The process of attenuating or stripping fibers that is done before you sit at the wheel or spindle to draft and make yarn.

Ratio

The number of times the flyer whorl spins in relation to the drive wheel. It helps to determine how much twist will go into a yarn.

Rolag

A roll of fiber made with handcards; essential for a traditionally spun woolen yarn.

Roving

Carded fibers that are in a long strand (as opposed to a batt).

Scotch tension

A single-drive wheel where the flyer is driven and the bobbin is braked.

Single drive

A type of wheel with a drive band that drives either the whorl or the bobbin but not both. There is a brake on either the bobbin or the flyer whorl in order to make the bobbin and flyer spin at different speeds.

Singles yarn

A yarn that is not plied.

Sliver

A carded preparation thinner than roving that is generated as an intermediate step in commercial spinning.

Staple

The length of an individual fiber from cut end to tip, or a lock from cut end to tip.

S-twist

Counterclockwise twist.

Top

A fiber preparation in which all the fibers are all parallel and the same length; essential for a traditionally spun worsted yarn. Hand-combed top preserves the orientation of each fiber so that the tip end is always presented first. Commercial top is a machine-produced variant in which the tip and cut ends are intermingled, and the fibers are pressed to subdue some of the crimp.

Tpi

Twists per inch.

Woolen

Yarn spun from a carded preparation where fibers are not parallel, with twist actively entering the drafting zone. Woolen yarns are loftier and fuzzier than their worsted counterparts. Also refers to techniques used to produce woolen yarns and to preparations appropriate for spinning woolen.

Worsted

Yarn spun from combed top where all the fibers are aligned parallel and where twist only enters already-drafted fibers held under tension. Worsted yarns are denser and smoother and can be of any thickness. Also refers to techniques used to produce worsted yarns and to preparations appropriate for worsted spinning.

Wpi

Wraps per inch.

Ypp

Yards per pound.

Z-twist

Clockwise twist.

resources

Amos, Alden. *The Alden Amos Big Book of Handspinning: Being a Compendium of Information, Advice, and Opinion on the Noble Art & Craft.* Loveland, Colorado: Interweave, 2001.

Casey, Maggie. *Start Spinning: Everything You Need to Know to Make Great Yarn.* Loveland, Colorado: Interweave, 2008.

Fournier, Nola, and Jane Fournier. *In Sheep's Clothing: A Handspinner's Guide to Wool.* Loveland, Colorado: Interweave, 1996; paperback reissue, 2003.

Varney, Diane. *Spinning Designer Yarn.* Loveland, Colorado: Interweave, 1987; reissue, 2003.

Rules of Thumb

To make something from a pattern using handspun yarn, look at the yardage requirements and the type of yarn. For a worsted-weight sweater with a 42" chest, the pattern may require 1,600 yards of yarn. If you estimate that you can produce 1,200 yards of worsted-weight yarn from 1 pound of wool, I would buy 1½ or 2 pounds of yarn to include enough for sampling.

Yarn Weights and Measurements

This handy guide will give you an indication of what kind of yarn you have spun and how it can best be used.

WPI (wraps per inch)	Type of Yarn	YPP (yards per pound)
8 or less	Super Bulky	400–500
10	Bulky	600–800
12	Worsted	900–1,200
14	Sport/DK	1,200–1,800
16	Fingering	1,800–2,400
18+	Lace	2,500+

What can I make?

In general, the following quantities of wool will be enough to knit most projects.

4 ounces (113 grams)	hat, socks, mittens
8 ounces (227 grams)	small vest, baby sweater, scarf, lace shawl
12 ounces (340 grams)	vest, child's sweater, large shawl
1 pound (454 grams)	small sweater, large vest
2 pounds (907 grams)	women's large-size sweater

index

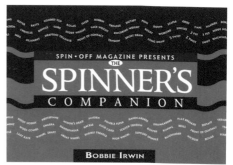